RE-IMAGINING
AMERICAN
CATHOLICISM

ALSO AVAILABLE IN VINTAGE SPECIALS

A Changing Israel: The New Political, Economic
and Social Realities in Israel Today
by Peter Grose (A Council on Foreign Relations Book)

Endless War: How We Got Involved
in Central America—and What Can Be Done
by James Chace

The Fallacy of Star Wars:
Why Space Weapons Can't Protect Us
by The Union of Concerned Scientists

Famine: A Man-Made Disaster?
by The Independent Commission on
International Humanitarian Issues
with an Introduction by Robert McNamara

Nuclear Proliferation Today:
The Spread of Nuclear Weapons 1984
by Leonard Spector   (A Carnegie Endowment Book)

Psychological Operations in Guerrilla Warfare:
The CIA's Nicaragua Manual
with essays by Aryeh Neier and Joanne Omang

The Russians and Reagan: How the Russians
Perceive Reagan's Foreign Policy
by Strobe Talbott (A Council on Foreign Relations Book)
with an introduction by Cyrus Vance

RE-IMAGINING AMERICAN CATHOLICISM

THE AMERICAN BISHOPS
AND THEIR PASTORAL
LETTERS

EUGENE KENNEDY

VINTAGE BOOKS
A DIVISION OF RANDOM HOUSE
NEW YORK

A Vintage Original, October 1985
First Edition
Copyright © 1985 by Eugene Kennedy
All rights reserved under International and Pan-American
Copyright Conventions. Published in the United States
by Random House, Inc., New York, and simultaneously
in Canada by Random House of Canada Limited, Toronto.

Library of Congress Cataloging in Publication Data
Kennedy, Eugene C.
Re-imagining American Catholicism.
1. Catholic Church–United States–Bishops–
Political activity. I. Title.
BX1407.P63K46   1985   262'.12'0973   85-40144
ISBN 0-394-74093-9 (pbk.)

Manufactured in the United States of America
Cover Photo: © 1985, Odette Lupis

MY WIFE SARA AND I

DEDICATE THIS BOOK

TO

JOHN FRANCIS CARDINAL DEARDEN

ACKNOWLEDGMENTS

I would like to thank Rosann Ward-Dawson for suggesting the writing of this book. I would be remiss not to thank Edward Klein, editor of the *New York Times Magazine,* and Ken Emerson, articles editor of that magazine, for proposing the topic to me in the first place. This book grew out of a piece I wrote for the *Times Magazine* and portions of that article appear in this manuscript.

Many people have cooperated generously as I researched this subject. These include the press officers of the United States Catholic Conference: Russ Shaw, Father Kenneth Doyle, William Ryan, and, especially, Robert Wonderly.

No one can write about American Catholic history without expressing gratitude to Monsignor John Tracy Ellis, an extraordinary man and scholar.

I would also like to thank Dan Kane, Michael Grace, S.J., Sister Rita Stalzer, C.S.J., Nina Polcyn Moore, and, of course, my secretary, Mary Louise Schniedwind. My most profound gratitude goes to the dean of American researchers on Catholic bishops, Dr. Frank J. Kobler.

CONTENTS

xi

Bɪꜱʜᴏᴘꜱ govern the particular churches entrusted to them as the vicars and ambassadors of Christ. This they do by their counsel, exhortations, and example, as well, indeed, as by their authority and sacred power. This power they use only for the edification of their flock in truth and holiness remembering that he who is greater should become as the lesser and he who is the more distinguished, as the servant (cf. Luke 22:26–27). This power, which they personally exercise in Christ's name, is proper, ordinary, and immediate, although its exercise is ultimately regulated by the supreme authority of the Church, and can be circumscribed by certain limits, for the advantage of the Church or of the faithful. In virtue of this power, bishops have the sacred right and the duty before the Lord to make laws for their subjects to pass judgment on them, and to moderate everything pertaining to the ordering of worship and the apostolate.

The pastoral office or the habitual and daily care of the sheep is entrusted to them completely. Nor are they to be regarded as vicars of the Roman Pontiff, for they exercise an authority which is proper to them, and are quite correctly called "prelates," heads of the people whom they govern. Their power, therefore, is not destroyed by the supreme and universal power. On the contrary it is affirmed, strengthened and vindicated thereby, since the Holy Spirit unfailingly preserves the form of government established by Christ the Lord in His Church.

Since he is sent by the Father to govern His family, a bishop must keep before his eyes the example of the Good Shepherd, who came not to be ministered unto but to minister (cf. Mt. 20:28; Mk. 10:45), and to lay down His life for His sheep (cf. John 10:11). Taken from among men, and himself beset with weakness, he is able to have compassion on the ignorant and erring (cf. Heb. 5:1–2). Let him not refuse to listen to his subjects, whom he cherishes as his true son and exhorts to cooperate readily with him. As having one day to render to God an account for their souls (cf. Heb. 13:17), he takes care of them by his prayer, preaching, and all the works of charity, and not only of them, but also of those who are not yet of the one flock. For these also are commended to him in the Lord.

Since, like Paul the Apostle, he is debtor to all men, let him be ready to preach the gospel to all (cf. Romans 1:14–15) and to urge his faithful to apostolic and missionary activity. For their part, the faithful must cling to their bishop, as the Church does to Christ, and Jesus Christ to the Father, so that everything may harmonize in unity, and abound to the glory of God (cf. Cor. 4:15).

DOCUMENTS OF VATICAN II
Lumen Gentium No. 27.

RE-IMAGINING
AMERICAN
CATHOLICISM

INTRODUCTION:
THE AMERICAN BISHOPS AND THEIR PASTORAL LETTERS

It is November 1980. Ronald Reagan, buoyed by his first landslide presidential election victory, looks toward the White House from his California home, eager to implement his twofold vision of weakening government's regulatory stranglehold on business while strengthening its grip on the fierce arrows of military defense. Across the continent the nation's Roman Catholic bishops, at their annual meeting in Washington, D.C., vote to begin preparatory work on two pastoral letters, one on nuclear war, the other on the American economy. The relationship between the President and the bishops, once as comfortably understanding of each other as, say, the country club president and his board of directors, has not been the same since.

Not long into his first term, the genially smiling

President was puzzled not only to find these Catholic bishops leading the loyal opposition to his Central American policies but, through pastoral letters, challenging his philosophy on nuclear arms and preparing to take issue with aspects of his economic program. Had these religious leaders been radicalized like the priests who mixed Marxism with gunpowder in the mountains of the Third World? Catholics who had voted in great numbers for the country's oldest president cheered as he began to chip away the Jackson Pollock–like drippings that had obscured their beloved Norman Rockwell canvas of America. They blinked in uncertain reaction, however, as the first full generation of post–Vatican Council II American bishops marked their assumption of authority by systematically questioning the new administration's manner of implementing cherished articles of Republican faith: anti-Communism, nuclear defense strategy, and the freedom of the free-enterprise system.

If the members of their own flocks were surprised to find their bishops drawn out of their safe gray ecclesiastical preserves into the klieg-lighted arena of international media attention, non-Catholics were astounded and variously aroused by what seemed the sudden intrusion of ecclesiastical leaders into issues judged by their critics as either beyond their competence or none of their business at all. Others, both Catholic and non-Catholic, including such distinguished figures as former ambassador to Russia George Kennan, applauded the bishops' careful examination of the moral lineaments of major national issues, admiring their purpose and courage even when they did not completely agree with them.

Once only occasional actors on the evening television news—ordinarily solemn, bespectacled, mostly Irish faces above starched white collars—speaking out against abortion or for federal funding for parochial schools, they are now familiar figures to viewers as well as to readers of newspapers and national magazines. Their pilgrimage into the focus of ambivalent public attention on an agenda that transcends partisan Catholic interests has demanded great adjustments both for them and for the nation. Whence these ecclesiastical leaders? Little more than a decade earlier, they had viewed the peace movement at a cautious distance (then FBI Director J. Edgar Hoover reportedly offered agency summaries on activist priests to members of the hierarchy), had supported the American presence in Vietnam in one of their statements, and busied themselves largely with intramural questions, such as whether Catholics could receive the Eucharist in the hand or not. They seemed to justify the appraisal offered by Richard Cardinal Cushing, the late archbishop of Boston, during the 1960 presidential campaign. The outspoken prelate told Joseph P. Kennedy, nervous about rumors that many bishops favored Richard M. Nixon over his son, "Don't worry, a lot of my confreres are Republican, and they pick the wrong side all the time."

It was, after all, no small reaction early in 1983 for

National Security Adviser William P. Clark, a former seminarian known in the Reagan administration as Mr. Catholic, to address a seven-page critique to Chicago's Joseph Cardinal Bernardin of the second draft of the pastoral letter on nuclear war being prepared by a small committee of bishops under the latter's chairmanship. Clark simultaneously released the document to the press in what was interpreted as an effort to influence public opinion, and the bishops' deliberations on the matter. Bernardin's committee calmly accepted the letter as a contribution, along with the testimony it had taken from scores of officials and experts, in helping them to shape their final version of a document, passed a few months later, that not only ruled out the moral acceptability of nuclear war, but also questioned nuclear deterrence as the foundation for long-term strategy of keeping the peace, and called for a "bi-lateral, verifiable" nuclear freeze.

Leading prelates, including Joseph Cardinal Bernardin, criticized the president's Central American policies early in Reagan's first term. This was underscored in a gentlemanly way early in 1984 on the specific point of the U.S. mining of Nicaraguan harbors, at a White House briefing for a delegation headed by the current president of the National Conference of Catholic Bishops (NCCB), James W. Malone of Youngstown, Ohio. President Reagan found these bishops loyal and courteous in their mannered dissent, but it represented a great change from that era in which the late cardinal-archbishops of New York,

Francis J. Spellman and Terence J. Cooke, as heads of what is called the Military Ordinariate, could be counted on for patriotic affirmation and support in difficult moments of national endeavor against Communist enemies. Government officials soon came to perceive the bishops, as one Washington columnist told a member of the bishops' staff, as their main obstacle to direct intervention in the Caribbean basin.

Frustrated by these experiences with what they had expected to be a somewhat passive and pious group —welcome for invocations but not advice on policy —a top White House adviser reacted to the news that the bishops had begun work on a pastoral letter on the nation's economy by reminding associates of their poor timing in dealing with both the nuclear letter and Central America and that "we had better be out front on this one." He wondered if Catholic business executives around the country could not begin to educate their bishops on the morally acceptable nature of the capitalist system. Perhaps they "should take a bishop out to lunch."

Within weeks a group of lay Catholics, headed by former Treasury Secretary William Simon, independently organized themselves to write a response to the bishops' economic letter, anticipated by one of them at the time as a probable "hatchet job" on business interests. Their brief document, issued a week before the first draft of the bishops' letter was made public, strongly defended capitalism as a sound and proven producer of the wealth needed for a successful economy. It seemed mild in comparison to the previews that had already appeared in such magazines as *Forbes* and *Fortune*. The latter grumpily asserted that the bishops would opt for socialistic measures because "socialism gives them a role to play, while capitalism —reliance on impersonal market forces—leaves them out in the cold." Indeed, these critiques correctly caught the tone—part anguish, part exasperation— with which many business executives and journalists greeted the first draft at its November release.

Such developments were counterpointed by the staggered beat of reactions among American Catholics at large and their journalistic observers, and by curial officials in the Vatican. Some believers, feeling that the once familiar territory of their faith had still not been cleared of the mines seeded in it by Vatican II, were unsure where to step. In their memory the Church resembled Mont St. Michel at dawn, a romantic and commanding eminence they valued precisely because it seemed to be raised on eternal and immutable foundations. They also remembered the bigger-than-life personalities of long-dead churchmen who knew how to act as princes of the Church: Spellman of New York, William O'Connell of Boston, and George Mundelein of Chicago. They had ruled as confidently as transplanted Renaissance monarchs, demanding absolute obedience from their flocks as they fought for Catholic respectability in Protestant America. Many Catholics had already experienced enough difficulty with the Mass translated into English and with once rigid doctrine oozing, as they saw it, into protoplasm. Some, after being trained to accept Church teaching and authority without question, felt a more profound disorientation, now to be called upon, like audience members urged onto the stage at an experimental theater, to participate in moral debates about nuclear war and the economy.

While many other Catholics spoke enthusiastically of their Church's new expectations that they would assume thought-provoking responsibilities, others confessed to a sense of "personal estrangement" and "philosophical hurt" that the bishops, seemingly without warning, had stepped out of their pulpits and into the middle of what they considered their own proper secular sphere. This was particularly true for Catholics who felt that in becoming successful within the free-enterprise system—it is estimated that as many as a third of the heads of the *Fortune* 500 companies are practicing Catholics—they had accomplished nothing less than what their Church had educated and urged them to do with their lives. Some reported feelings of alienation similar to those experienced by certain Catholic members of the military, who reacted angrily at their bishops for casting, in their nuclear arms letter, at least a beige shadow across their careers in the defense of their country, a calling once esteemed just a shade beneath that to the priesthood and religious life in spiritual nobility.

Analysts of American Catholic behavior openly wondered at the bishops' motives in tackling such projects as nuclear war and capitalism. Were they, more than one group of newspaper editors asked, seeking new constituencies through these pastoral letters? Did the bishops feel that they had lost touch with many middle-class Catholics who had, in the generation after Vatican II, become, in beliefs and practices, such as church attendance and the practice of birth control, almost indistinguishable from their Protestant or pagan neighbors? Were they searching for a new base for their political strength among the huge numbers of the poor and otherwise disenfranchised in America? Many commentators, including the syndicated columnist Carl Rowan, strongly criticized the bishops for withholding their draft of the economic pastoral until after Election Day 1984, suggesting that their failure to reveal their feelings about the Reagan economic plans contributed to the disastrous defeat of the Democratic Party and, therefore, to the continuing distress of the very poor, whose cause they claimed to champion.

Roman curial officials, prompted by letter-writing campaigns orchestrated by Catholics alarmed by what they considered a collapse of authority and discipline within their Church, also voiced concerns about the manner in which the American bishops prepared their pastoral letters. In a 1983 article, the University of Louvain professor Michel Schooyans implied that the bishops' approach, with its extensive consultation, weakened the magisterium, or papal teaching authority. Schooyans referred to "the troublesome things coming from the North American Episcopal Conference's consistent publishing of its mischief making" and indicted its practice of working through several versions of its statements as "running the risk of sowing confusion and division." Schooyans was thought to have expressed the sentiments of Bishop Jan Schotte, a close adviser of Pope John Paul II, whom he accompanied on his 1979 visit to the United States.

A 1984 interview with Joseph Cardinal Ratzinger, head of the Vatican department of the Congregation of the Doctrine of the Faith, known once as the Holy Office in *Jesus,* an Italian Catholic magazine published in Milan, fed the already intense speculation about the skepticism of some Vatican administrators about the style of the American bishops' conference. The German cardinal, a trained theological contemporary of the liberal Swiss scholar Hans Küng, suggested that if national conferences of bishops became too independent, they might give the impression of diluting the unity of the Church's teaching authority. Ratzinger also criticized American theologians for allegedly surrendering to, rather than confronting, the values of the surrounding culture.

The influential prelate expressed a common, almost chronic curial misgiving about the U.S. bishops: The Americans function like the superpower that is their host nation; they possess the wealth, the numbers, the confidence, and perhaps something like the enthusiastic naïveté of the New World. They therefore also bear the weight of every European hesitation and uneasiness about Americans in general. There is, however, nothing new about this Henry James scenario. Almost a century before, American bishops had been accused by curial officials of being too enamored of democratic ways. One of the leading prelates of the time, Archbishop John Ireland of St. Paul, was thought to have been denied a cardinal's hat for being too closely associated with a suspected brand of heresy condemned as "Americanism." Bishops in the United States were considered too given to the active virtues, a charge whose hundred-year-old echo can be heard clearly in the present suspicion of what is now termed their activism.

The present position of American bishops cannot be understood aside from their commitment to the principle of collegiality that was enunciated clearly by Vatican II. "Collegiality" refers to that method of Church governance that acknowledges and enlarges the role of the world's bishops, defining their authority as derived from God and not doled out by the pope. While the supreme authority of the pope was not thereby denied, Vatican II did restore a balance in the scale of relationships between the bishops and the pope that had been tipped strongly in favor of the latter by the aborted Vatican Council I (1869–1870). The latter council had defined the infallibility of the pope and departed from Rome, its work unfinished, as the Eternal City, the last vestige of once extensive papal landholdings, came under attack from the forces of Victor Emmanuel.

Although the pope at the time, Pius IX, saw his worldly empire dissolve, he employed the mysterious aura of his newly acclaimed theological infallibility to elevate his spiritual and psychological claims on the

imaginations of Catholics and non-Catholics alike.
This pope, who ruled through the tumultuous central
third of the century, had already done much to make
Rome the magnetic pole to which all Catholics felt
an increasing attraction and deferential obedience.
Pius IX left a Church whose power was profoundly
centralized in Rome and a papacy that, shorn of its
earthly power, seemed thereby to tighten its grasp on
spiritual authority.

His successors accepted and expanded the regal dignity of their office, ruling as absolute monarchs well
past the middle of the twentieth century. The papal
shadow lengthened, casting an obscuring darkness
over the practical role and function of the bishops in
the universal church. Vatican II, called by Pope John
XXIII in 1959, set about restoring the authority intrinsic to the office of a bishop while not diminishing
that of the pope. The bishops now in power have been
deeply imbued with a renewed sense of the authority
proper to their office and their obligations to exercise
it, especially through collegial relationships with their
fellow bishops. These theological headwaters are the
ultimate source of the newly expressed pastoral energy of the world's bishops in general, and of the
American bishops in particular.

The bishops' apparent conflicts with the Reagan administration should not be identified as items written
boldly into a carefully crafted political agenda. While
the bishops have for many years had clear objectives

for governmental action, including their broad program against abortion and their search for federal aid to the Catholic school system, their clashes with the White House on nuclear war and economic policies have been by-products of their acceptance of their collegial responsibilities and the process essential to their exercise as they deal as pastors with major problems. They did not choose Reagan or his policies as specific targets; they would have carried out their discussions without regard to which party was in office. That the prelates have explored nuclear strategy and the harmful side effects of the free-enterprise system in a detailed, public, and newsworthy manner is fundamentally a function of their practical efforts to implement the role of bishops as it was defined in Vatican II. The bishops, as will be discussed later, are men of duty, and they perceive collegial deliberations as a pressing theological imperative.

The American bishops have replaced the authoritarian style that seemed natural to many of their colorful predecessors with procedures that seek not so much to speak the last word to settle issues as to utter the first words to open far-ranging discussions on the moral aspects of serious contemporary issues. Their sense of duty about the collegial process undergirds the determination with which, despite enormous pressures, criticism, and efforts to manipulate them, they carry out their obligations as bishops. Several advantages arise from their self-understanding and from the process to which they have so thoroughly committed themselves.

The Catholic bishops of the United States draw great strength from what, in another way, is an exhausting exercise in working together as a cooperative body. Their theological convictions about their links, through what is known as apostolic succession, to the authority of the Church's first bishop, the apostle Peter, deliver to them both a sense of confidence about their episcopal mission and a certain insulation against even the harshest criticism, which they expect and may read in their spiritual tradition as a sign that they are on the right track. They sense, at some level, that they are part of a vast, somewhat mysterious, somewhat mystical organization that has found a way, amidst the wreckage of long-forgotten kingdoms, to survive both time and chance.

These are powerful elements of what may be termed the "episcopal ideal," that set of beliefs about themselves and their calling that is far older and more powerful in its effects than the mystique that reinforces the membership of other ongoing collectivities, such as the wandering remnants of royalty, or relatively recently developed entities as the French Academy or the United States Senate. The elements of this highly effective "ideal" will be discussed in detail later, but their imprint on the psychology of the American Catholic bishops is extremely significant in the way they conduct themselves during this passage of history.

Collegial processes resemble a rich medicinal pack that draws out of those to whom it is applied an almost dogged capacity for meeting, listening, discussing, revising, amending, voting, and starting the whole thing over again at first light. An enormous power, never grasped by flashily charismatic leaders, is delivered to those who, like legislators well versed in the intricacies of bills and Roberts Rules of Order, embrace the unglamorous drudgery of translating even the greatest causes and noblest ideals into practice in the everyday experience of the community. Any successful institutionalization of power depends on a cohort that embraces and masters its legislative and administrative machinery. The Catholic bishops of the United States have established a strong presence in current affairs because their way of seeking consensus statements in their pastoral letters involves them in equivalent ecclesiastical behaviors.

The men who become bishops identify with the very procedures by which they invite all those from their own Catholic tradition—and from others as well—to accept a share of responsibility for reflecting on the moral implications of the significant issues that preoccupy the world. They also command a network across which these deliberations can be communicated —the parishes, schools, diocesan newspapers, and other organizational tools put into place over the years—and from which they can also receive feedback. The density of the administrative realities of what might be termed the American Catholic enterprise provides them with a unique and firm base. The bishops have a bully pulpit from which to speak.

This is abetted by the fascination that the public has

for the clergy in general and for those of the Catholic Church in particular. The mystique that attaches to the procedures and personnel of the Church remains strong, as is evidenced by its frequent use in novels and plays. The dramatic possibilities of such a group of clergymen are enhanced when they are challenged by the government administration in any country. It has been no less so in the United States in recent years. The tactics of the White House have not been particularly subtle or effective and have, in the long run, contributed greatly to the attention that has been given to the bishops and their pastoral letters.

The emphasis on process over personality in the administration of the American Catholic Church, while a logical outgrowth of the theology of the bishopric enunciated at Vatican II, also eases the tensions that have periodically arisen in the Church in the United States when issues have been subordinated to the great figures who championed or opposed them. The essentially collaborative nature of the NCCB as it was established immediately after Vatican II was not accidental but, as will be discussed in the next chapter, the outcome of the then contested vision of its first president, John F. Dearden, the now retired cardinal-archbishop of Detroit. The pastoral letters that have attracted the attention of the entire country in the eighties might have been filed and forgotten, as so many of them had been since the bishops first started issuing them in 1792, if Dearden had not made the formation of a working conference of bishops his main objective in the latter part of the sixties. While speculation about the influence of various personalities within the Church continues, it no longer constantly threatens to overshadow the process of collegiality whose dynamics currently govern the bishops' working agenda.

It should also be noted that the use of the process of collegiality in governing the Church in the United States has preserved the authority of the bishops at a time when it could easily have been permanently compromised. Collegiality, which involves those in authority in a mode of administration very different from the quasi-authoritarianism of the Church's heavily monarchic period, emphasizes the spiritual rather than the legal aspects of membership in the Church. This permits many questions to be dealt with in what is termed a pastoral manner, that is, one in which the teaching of the Church is applied with a respect and understanding for the human situation—a realization of sinfulness as a shared state—while it confronts people with their obligation to take responsibility for the moral dimension of their existences. The equation is no longer a simple one, in which bishops exact blind obedience to absolute commands. The pastoral approach does not make authority and obedience issues that overwhelm the moral content of the questions under discussion, such as nuclear war and aspects of the economy.

The American Catholic bishops, the letter on nuclear arms completed and the one on the economy awaiting its final vote, find themselves members of a strong, well-organized episcopal conference that is currently under the careful appraisal of widely different groups both inside and outside the church. Archbishop Rembert G. Weakland of Milwaukee, who began his career in the Church as a Benedictine monk, chairs the committee of bishops that has developed the pastoral letter "Catholic Social Teaching and the U.S. Economy." "We are living," he says thoughtfully, "at a time in which we must re-imagine the Catholic Church. It isn't easy but it is necessary for every Catholic. We must examine our own moral convictions, work them through in the light of the Gospel so that we hold them deeply for ourselves. In these pastoral letters, the bishops are not writing for political reasons, but to begin serious discussions on the major issues of our times."

He acknowledges that the American Catholic Church has, to the puzzlement of some believers, extended its focus beyond their personal lives to their professional lives, identifying them as organically related and bringing an end to the days when religion could be considered a private devotional affair, a garden walled off from the larger world. "That is part," he says, as if speaking for his brother bishops, who are charting new courses for American Catholicism and its function in the national culture, "of the re-imagining that must take place."

ONE

WHO ARE
THE AMERICAN
CATHOLIC
BISHOPS?

T HE history of the present organization of the American Catholic bishops is an archaeological dig from whose sides glint the edges and shards of other times and other worlds: Catholicism climbing with immigrant determination over the edge of the twentieth century, scarred by its struggles to become accepted as a belief system and a way of life congenial to and supportive of democratic principles; Catholicism at the middle of this century, rich in schools, churches, and seminaries, closing the immigrant phase of its experience as, after long denial, one of its sons pursued America's final seal of acceptance through seeking the presidency; Catholicism as the twenty-first century comes into view, well assimilated into the culture, its bishops suddenly sounding like prophets, a community hesitant about its participatory role in a Church working through its aftermath adjustments to the reforms of Vatican II. The genealogical line of the bishops trails down through the layers of American Catholic history, a crimson thread binding them together, symbolizing authority, tradition, and the spiritual and psychological energies that support the Church both as parish and as a highly complex, international organization.

As the present century opened, the bishops presided over an American Catholic Church that was still technically a "missionary" community in the eyes of Roman officials. It would not be freed from supervision by the Congregation for the Propagation of the Faith until 1908. When the Church was first established, the curia, following the ancient model of Roman Empire organization, had divided it into provinces, in which smaller dioceses clustered around a principal archdiocese in a major city. The archbishops of the country met every year to discuss their common concerns as well as their relationships with Roman authorities. Even a century ago curial administrators displayed the same classic European skepticism about America and its capacity for self-governance that their successors express today.

It was at Rome's insistence that the bishops convened plenary councils, formal gatherings of the nation's bishops and their advisers, the most famous of which was held in Baltimore in 1884. This historical meeting was, after protests, presided over not by an Italian delegate, as Rome originally wished, but by the archbishop of Baltimore, James Gibbons. It has been speculated that the bishops of America, perhaps because of the reluctance of some of them to support the doctrine of infallibility at Vatican I, were subject to close curial supervision even though American Catholics were well known even at that time for their affection for and devotion to the pope. The council's agenda was, therefore, prepared in the Vatican. The decrees it issued implemented largely unifying regulations on a wide variety of matters ranging from Catholic education to the discipline of the clergy. One of its most important was that requiring parishes to build Catholic schools.

At the time, the bishops and clergy, along with the religious nuns and brothers who staffed the growing school system, were frequently the only educated persons in their immigrant communities and became greatly respected figures in the Catholic culture. Industrious, bent on respectability, the Catholic people wanted their bishops to live as well as the mayor or the head of the mill in their town. He was, after all, the symbol of the religious belief by which they were regularly identified and judged; if he could stand on an equal plane with the movers and shakers of the community, they could stand vicariously next to him. One must remember the suspicion with which Catholics were then viewed and the history of anti-Catholic activities in nineteenth-century America. The American Protective Association was formed to safeguard Protestant America from Catholic influences, going so far as to advocate the denial of employment to Catholics in the United States. It was only by a thin margin of votes that an amendment to the U.S. Constitution requiring attendance at public schools and denying financial aid to any religious institution, supported by President Grant, was defeated.

The bishop, not then a member of any well-organized conference with his fellow bishops, was by well-established theological tradition and practice the sole authority in his jurisdiction. He operated chiefly in relationship to Rome and its congregations and to the pope himself, who, as previously noted, had firmly reinforced his place in the world's imagination as the supreme ruler of late-nineteenth-century Catholicism and was the direct and willing recipient of its obedience, loyalty, and affection.

Indeed, the declaration of infallibility Pius IX had accepted in July 1870 as the troops of Victor Emmanuel, the man who would be king of a reunified Italy, massed outside the gates of Rome, sent tremors radiating across Western Europe. Many non-Catholic leaders feared the political repercussions of the doctrine of infallibility on the loyalty of their own Catholic subjects. Britain's Prime Minister William Gladstone issued a stately volume, termed an "expostulation," *The Vatican Decrees in Their Bearing on Civil Allegiance,* to which John Henry Cardinal Newman made a careful and thorough response. It was typical of the age that a single prelate would stand as an individual spokesman in any country to enunciate or to defend the rights of the Catholic people. If Newman was that person in England, James Cardinal Gibbons of Baltimore was his counterpart in the United States. Baltimore was considered the first, or primatial-like, see, and for a half century Gibbons, somewhat like Cardinal Spellman in a later generation, was the principal mediating spokesman for that straining, muscular, not quite yet settled cultural phenomenon known as American Catholicism. A more aggressive American prelate was St. Paul's Archbishop John Ireland, who involved himself with Teddy Roosevelt–like enthusiasm in a startling variety of activities, including an effort through his personal mediation to head off the 1898 war with Spain.

Pope Pius IX, who reigned from 1846 to 1878, imposed his own character and expectations on the enormous number of bishops he appointed during his longest of papal terms. Democratic in his earliest years in office, his warm personality made him popular among people and bishops alike. Treasured Rome with its white-figured pope walking among the people became the goal of every sophisticated pilgrimage, secular as well as spiritual, in that rapidly expanding era of transportation and communication. Pio Nono, as he was affectionately called, projected a great personality in a world already crowded with extraordinary personages as he impressed his interpretation of the papacy as clearly as his fisherman's ring into a wax seal on a world just awakening to modern times.

Some of America's bishops had hesitated to vote for

infallibility (one of the two *non placet* votes was, in fact, cast by Bishop Edward Fitzgerald of Little Rock, Arkansas, and some other Americans left early to avoid the vote), but within a relatively short time they pledged their loyalty to the pope, now a more dominant figure than ever in relationship to them and Catholicism in the United States. Fitzgerald, exemplifying the quickly marshaled allegiance that characterizes American bishops even today, made his pledge of fidelity to the pope immediately after the vote, saying, "Now I believe." This readiness to give their assent to papal authority, at an unknown interior cost to themselves, has been an enduring quality in the American college of bishops. They have consistently put the Church, conceived of by them as an overriding mystical reality, and the pope, revered as one bearing in his office the seed of the authority anchoring that Church in time and eternity, at the center of what they understand as their calling as bishops. Today's collegially oriented bishops understand their own authority as linked inseparably to the pope's and view their own functioning together in a national conference as a way of expressing their unity with his purposes within the particular conditions of their own culture. No constellation of legislators, executives, not even Japanese factory managers, can rival them in well-practiced and efficacious loyalty to the organization of which they are a part.

This loyalty, then as now held up to the light by haggling curial officials as if it were suspect goods,

identifies today's bishops as blood brothers of their predecessors. Unlike the latter in many ways—the present
bishops have little taste for authoritarian perquisites—
they strongly resemble them in their devotion to the
Holy See and their readiness to demonstrate that loyalty even in the face of savage storms of criticism and
misunderstanding. This powerful dynamic has been a
constant at every stage of their transformation from
shepherds of immigrant flocks on a missionary continent into the most highly organized and powerful conference of prelates in the universal Church.

At the time of World War I, American bishops still
presided over communities struggling to find their
rightful place in American society. It was a gilded age
of authoritarianism in which the bristling figures of
such prelates as William Cardinal O'Connell of Boston and George Cardinal Mundelein of Chicago
crowded the center stage of Catholic life in the
United States. Personality would dominate over institutional process for long years to come, but the first
identifiable organizational ancestor of the present
conference of bishops can be found in the National
Catholic War Council, established after the United
States entered World War I.

The administrative committee of this relatively
loose aggregate was chaired by Bishop Peter J. Mul-
doon of Rockford, Illinois. Its members offered a
prophecy of the activities of contemporary bishops as
they sketched in the first lines of what would become

the chart of their modern organization, a chart as complicated as the diagram of a clause-filled sentence. Shortly after the war, these bishops set themselves on a progressive track through issuing what has been described by historian Francis L. Broderick as "perhaps the most forward-looking social document ever to have come from an official Catholic agency in the United States." It clearly foreshadowed the 1984 draft of the pastoral letter on the economy both in its content and in the reception it received from the business community.

This statement differed from the present pastoral, however, in that it did not represent the collective thought of the bishops as much as their general intention to make a statement about the desirable goals of postwar reconstruction. It was composed, in fact, of the unedited notes of an undelivered speech of Father John A. Ryan, a liberal social thinker who would later influence the policies of Franklin D. Roosevelt's New Deal. Determined to do something constructive, the bishops achieved a reputation for liberal thought by supporting a document that may have gone beyond the personal convictions of many of them. No bishop ever repudiated the statement, however, and it came to stand as a kind of Magna Carta of the social ideals of the American Church. Through it the bishops placed social action permanently and prominently on the agenda of their pastoral and organizational concerns.

The Catholic bishops of the nineteenth century had

given notable support to the burgeoning labor movement in the United States, especially in an age of
Church suspicion of secret organizations and socialism
in any form, through their defense of the Knights of
Labor and its Catholic leader, Terence V. Powderly.
Similar organizations in Canada had been criticized
by the Vatican. Archbishop Gibbons of Baltimore,
named a cardinal in 1886, used the occasion of his
official investiture in Rome the next year to deliver
an address vindicating this pioneering union that was
the basis for the American Federation of Labor. The
bishops' endorsement of the labor movement—in
which many of their priests and people, including
Mary Harris, the legendary union organizer Mother
Jones, were frontline activists—remains illustrative of
the manner, perhaps more dutiful than passionate, in
which members of the American hierarchy have char-
acteristically involved themselves in social issues.

Historian James Roohan describes the leading bishops of the latter half of the nineteenth century as
generally conservative men whose reputation for liberal thinking derived chiefly from their support of the
Knights of Labor and of social thinker Henry
George's right to speak without censorship. Archbishop Ireland was a solid Republican who at the turn
of the century allowed the young priest John A. Ryan
to teach in the St. Paul Seminary "economic doctrines
and advocate reforms in which Ireland had no faith."
John Lancaster Spalding, bishop of Peoria, Illinois,
from 1877 to 1908, was considered the most intellec-

tual of the bishops of his period, but, according to Roohan, he "saw religion as peculiarly the property and the consolation of the poor, and, in accordance with traditional Catholic thought in the matter, regarded poverty and suffering, rightly understood, as opportunities for good." He and his fellow bishops emphasized "the primacy of the moral individual" and the conviction that individuals made institutions rather than the other way around. All bishops at the time, Roohan asserts, opposed state influence in private business affairs.

Although they reflect the traditions of an earlier time, these themes have remained within the American Catholic consciousness. They have resurfaced in recent criticisms of the present conference of bishops over the content and recommendations of their pastoral letters. That the bishops of the last century could publicly support movements that outran their own privately conservative views illustrates a paradoxical but perennial truth about the episcopal personality. American bishops have almost always been highly intelligent men who can understand and incorporate positions they recognize as theoretically correct even before they fully accept them emotionally.

Except in rare cases, American bishops have felt a duty to inspect all sides of issues, and, therefore, to allow all interested parties in any discussion adequate opportunity to express themselves. It is currently evidenced in the extensive hearings conducted by the committees of bishops working on various pastoral letters. They regularly take testimony from people of widely differing convictions. In preparing the first draft of the economic pastoral, for example, the bishops listened to union leaders, business executives, government officials, and economists of every ideological stripe. This decidedly American trait, described by Roohan as an aspect of what he terms their "principled pragmatism," may derive from the typical fascicle of qualities—including dutifulness, fairness, and bureaucratic aptitude—found regularly in men chosen to be bishops. This willingness to entertain diverse opinions does not reflect the poet's love of ambivalence as much as the bishops' willed openness to the demands made on them from many sides. Their fate, in a sense, is to listen as much as it is to preach. This characteristic contributes to their ability to invest their energies into projects their heads tell them to carry out even before they can put their hearts fully into them.

The 1919 statement of the barely viable ancestor of the present conference of bishops contained recommendations urging the government to preserve many of the services that had been set up as emergency war measures, including the national labor board that had given support to labor's right to organize, collective bargaining, and the familial living wage. Although accepting the private ownership of capital, the bishops called for action to prevent the monopolistic control of commodities and also asked for "heavy taxation of incomes, excess profits and inheritances." A living wage, the bishops held, was only the minimum of what justice demanded. They concluded with references to the 1891 encyclical letter on labor of Pope Leo XIII, *Rerum Novarum,* and reminded employers of "the long-forgotten truth that wealth is stewardship."

The president of the National Association of Manufacturers complained to the aged Cardinal Gibbons that the statement was "partisan, pro-labor union socialist propaganda." Others, sniffing anarchy in the wind, linked the bishops with those who would overthrow the nation's institutions and cause chaos. Although it was not an official document of the bishops, it came to be perceived as embodying their program and legitimated the advanced teachings of Ryan as those supported by the Church. Non-Catholic liberals were amazed by the statement. Upton Sinclair referred to it as the "Catholic miracle," and Raymond Gram Swing wrote in *The Nation* of the remarkable social vision of the institution that "rightly or wrongly, has been reputed to be the most conservative."

The bishops had approved a program of social thinking far ahead of that of many Catholics. They further buttressed it and simultaneously laid down a preliminary design for their own future mission by petitioning the pope to make permanent their National Catholic War Council as the National Catholic Welfare Council. They funded, among other things, a social action department, the Washington office of which was to be run by Father John A. Ryan. The very elements that now guide the development of the bishops' pastoral on the economy were, therefore, put in place in 1919. The first national organization of bishops, although voluntary and without binding jurisdiction on its members, was established, along with an ongoing department that would provide the principles of progressive thought on which the bishops would base their social teaching for decades to come. That embryonic structure, whose very existence would be severely contested within the next few years, would emerge, transformed in status and authority by Vatican Council II, as the National Conference of Catholic Bishops. Its early history contained the genetic material that determined the course of its development and the guiding philosophy of its liberal social teaching, as well as the conflicts about its structure and function that have continued into the present time.

This new National Catholic Welfare Council did not please some bishops, who felt that its collective structure might impinge on their own independence in being, as the clerical saying of the day put it, "the boss in their own diocese." Dennis Cardinal Dougherty of Philadelphia and William Cardinal O'Connell of Boston led the fierce attack. The crisis occasioned by their discontent anticipated the contemporary criticisms, largely from curial officials, about the danger of episcopal conferences' overshadowing the rights of individual prelates. Indeed, some of the then reigning bishops resisted the idea of a conference as an agency of cooperative work, preferring to follow the traditions of earlier times, when their predecessors did their own business directly with Rome without involving themselves excessively with their American confreres. It is instructive to quote from a decree of the Consistorial Congregation, the Roman office in charge of bishops, of February 25, 1922:

In the United States of America, the custom has recently arisen that all diocesan ordinaries assemble . . . to treat of some matters which seemed to require assembled deliberation . . . In order to settle other matters . . . they have determined to establish a certain committee of bishops called the NCWC [National Catholic Welfare Council].

But now, because circumstances have changed, some bishops . . . have decided that the procedure and this establishment is no longer needed or useful; so they have asked the Holy See that steps be taken.

Decision: . . . such general meetings are not to be held anymore.

The dispute was resolved through negotiation between a group of bishops and Roman officials, but the tension of the discussions—and a classic example of American directness—survives in these sentences from a report written by Bishop Joseph Schrembs who helped negotiate the crisis. "They (i.e., the Holy See) are always talking about the autonomy of the single bishop. It's a smoke screen. What they mean is that it is easier to deal with one bishop than with a hierarchy." The decree was soon rescinded with the qualification that the organization's name be changed to the National Catholic Welfare Conference and that its nature be voluntary and its jurisdiction severely limited. The bishops also established a civil body, the National Catholic Welfare Conference, Inc., the antecedent to the United States Catholic Conference.

The National Catholic Welfare Conference became the instrument through which the bishops organized their work in the United States and through which they issued regular statements. Although some prelates, including Thomas E. Molloy of the large and important diocese of Brooklyn, New York, never attended its annual meetings, this confederation of bishops survived as the voice of organized American Catholicism for the next forty years.

John F. Dearden, a priest from Cleveland, was named bishop of Pittsburgh in 1948. Ten years later he was designated archbishop of Detroit in the first batch of American appointments made by Pope John XXIII after his election. Dearden would soon become the principal architect of the NCCB as it now exists. By his own admission, Dearden was transformed by his experience at Vatican II from the hard-line conservative positions that had earned him the nickname Iron John into a progressive leader, well versed in contemporary theology. His years of seasoning in the ranks of the bishops had acquainted him fully with the weakly organized national episcopate that was still excessively dominated by vivid and demanding individual personalities like Patrick Cardinal O'Boyle of Washington, D.C., and James Francis Cardinal McIntyre of Los Angeles. These men would, in fact, work successfully against Dearden's being named a cardinal in 1967, and he would receive the red hat two years later.

Dearden, however, possessed what bishops often describe as "credibility." He was the recipient of the generalized trust and practical confidence of his confreres. They felt that he had their interests and those of the Church at large always in view and that he would not deceive them or use his office in the service of personal ambition. It was no surprise that he was chosen as the first president of the newly structured NCCB when it was established, in accordance with the decrees of Vatican II, in 1966. One of his first moves was to request the release of a just-named auxiliary bishop of Atlanta, Joseph L. Bernardin, to be his principal administrative assistant. Now the cardinal-archbishop of Chicago, Bernardin is one of the most prominent leaders of contemporary American Catholicism and one of the chief advocates of collegial process over individual personality in the development of the bishops' pastoral letters.

Pressed to initiate a dramatic nationwide program of Vatican II renewal as he had in his own diocese, Dearden set for himself a more difficult and exacting goal—that of making the NCCB into a genuinely collaborative working organization. From his experience with Detroit's auto industry, Dearden had come to value the American genius for labor negotiation and felt that this could not only be incorporated into the spirit and practice of the new organization but might eventually be exported as a unique American contribution to other national churches. Dearden decided, in other words, to build, as the vehicle of collegiality, an effective bureaucracy that would respect the autonomy of each member bishop. He wanted the bishops to feel comfortable in and confident of this new organization as they gradually learned to work together on common church problems. Dearden understood that the theology of collegiality needed to sink foundations that were strong and deep enough to accommodate the stresses the bishops would inevitably experience as they slowly developed a new kind of fraternal interdependence in their pastoral work.

This NCCB is a canonical body, that is, one established by church law as a result of the decrees of Vatican II. Designed to deal mainly with internal church questions, such as worship and seminary education, it also participates in pro–life matters and, on occasion, issues statements about other political and social questions. The bishops constitute its membership, and the conference meets annually, usually in November in Washington, D.C. The bishops also established a counterpart civil organization, the United States Catholic Conference (USCC), in 1966, through which to address public issues in a systematic way. Its members are the bishops, but its structure includes a staff of priests and religious and lay persons. This body is organized around three departmental committees and three corresponding departments of communications, education, and social development and world peace. These, with subdivisions of their own, engage in activities that include preparing curriculum materials for Catholic schools and adult-education programs, writing articles for Catholic newspapers and journals, and representing the Church before the branches of the government. Both the NCCB and the USCC occupy the same Washington, D.C., offices. The principal officers of the organization are bishops elected for three year terms by the membership. A general secretary, now Monsignor Daniel F. Hoye, serves as the chief operating officer.

The bishops communicate officially in four ways: joint pastorals, formal statements, special messages, and resolutions and brief statements. A joint pastoral, such as the one on the American economy, can be issued only by the NCCB and requires the approval of two thirds of the membership. The rules, and the actual operational style employed in the letters on nuclear war and the economy, guarantee extensive opportunities for review and revision during the course of the development of such major pastoral statements. As in all organizations—the bishops employed Booz Allen as consultants in the bureaucratic planning, another evidence of their practical American bent—detailed policies regulate the other modes of communication to guarantee their origin and the character of the teaching authority they embody. Some critics of the conference structure suggest that the NCCB is roughly equivalent to the Senate and that the USCC corresponds to the senatorial staff. These observers claim that the staff members, whom they accuse of being classically "liberal" in their thinking, may exercise excessive influence in shaping episcopal documents because they play such a large role in preparing basic research materials. Still other critics, as will be discussed later, claim that a subtle but significant shift has occurred since the National Catholic Welfare Council became the National Conference of Catholic Bishops, asserting that the new organization has downplayed evangelization and stresses structural rather than personal change in offering solutions to the problems of the day.

As mentioned earlier, some Europeans take exception to the democratic procedures employed by the bishops in preparing the drafts of their most important letters. They insinuate that too much consultation can only lead to confusion about the location and unity of the Church's teaching authority. In any case, a generation after its establishment, the NCCB has transformed the manner in which its bishop members perceive themselves and work with one another. Their becoming identified as religious leaders to whom the culture has begun to pay attention if not completely to give heed is correlated with their practical organizational implementation of the theological principle of collegiality.

Working together, they carry out, in effect, public reflections on the moral aspects of issues that transcend religious affiliation. The collaborative and searching nature of their process has been a principal factor in drawing attention to their pastoral letters-in-the-making. The process took on new dynamism in the early 1980s because a new generation of post–Vatican II bishops had just come into major positions of ecclesiastical responsibility.

Joseph L. Bernardin, for example, became archbishop of Chicago in August 1982, and, as chairman of the committee of bishops already at work on the letter on nuclear war, brought new attention and prestige to that effort. After many years of practical experience, first as general secretary and then as president of the NCCB, he brought deep convictions about the urgency of the collegial process to his new and highly visible position. Another extraordinary man, Rembert G. Weakland, had been made archbishop of Milwaukee in 1977 after ten years as abbot primate of the Benedictine order. He brought to his chairmanship of the committee working on the economic pastoral a broad and unique experience of universal Catholicism and its struggles to come to terms with the collegial vision of Vatican II. These are but two of the leaders of the American Catholic Church who did their ecclesiastical apprenticeships during that strenuous era in which the Church adapted to the collegial modes dictated by the council. A conjunction of events—the assumption of authority by a new generation of bishops, the maturing of their consultative process, the counterpointing historical occurrences in national and international life—gave the pastoral letters of the bishops a new and undeniable relevancy.

Their process, which effectively shifts them from an authoritarian to a collegial position—they are raising questions instead of only giving final answers—is a central reason for their building experience of media attention. When everything is sorted out, this process—and the structures on which it depends—are the double focus of those who support and those who criticize the bishops. Clearly, the destiny of the process that defines them as bishops even as they use it to speak out—strongly American in its call for wide participation, strongly theological in its rootedness in Vatican II—is also a major element in the destiny of institutional Catholicism in America.

TWO

AMERICAN BISHOPS: INSTITUTIONAL MEN

THE Catholic bishops constitute a corporate presence in the national imagination. They are spoken of in the plural, are often seen on television or in the newspapers in groups, as, for example, on visits to the White House or Central America, and are frequently criticized as a body. This is not evidence of a deliberate strategy or of some new regulation resembling the old one that required nuns to travel in twos. Rather, it is a side effect of the development of their consciousness of themselves as members of a national episcopal conference. They have become accustomed to teamlike assignments and present themselves unself-consciously as collaborators as well as individuals in a way that would have been the exception rather than the rule just a generation ago. They have not abandoned their awareness of their own authority within their own dioceses, but the elaborated theology of Vatican II constantly reminds them that they possess that power precisely because they are members of a college of bishops. One cannot understand the American bishops without an appreciation of their sense of communion, through their episcopal office, with one another and with their brother bishops throughout the world, including the pope himself as the bishop of Rome. It is the foundation stone of their spiritual, personal, and collegial identity and the source of enormous strength and staying power for the institution they serve.

Speaking at a special meeting of the bishops held at Collegeville, Minnesota, in June 1982, John Cardinal Dearden carefully explored the question of the bishops' overlapping identities as members of this special college and as autonomous leaders of local dioceses. He cited *Lumen Gentium,* the Vatican II document that discusses collegiality: "The order of bishops is the successor of the college of the Apostles in their role as teachers and pastors, and in it the apostolic college is perpetuated. Together with their head, the Supreme Pontiff, and never apart from him, they have supreme and full authority over the universal Church; but this power cannot be exercised without the agreement of the Roman Pontiff."

Dearden's purpose was to encourage bishops to accept their collegial responsibilities in the NCCB as being complementary to rather than competitive with their individual diocesan concerns. He accented the theological roots of their power in a set of relationships that not only repeat those of Christ with his apostles but also extend them in time. These men had entered into an awesome and mysterious communion with the pope—and he with them—through their common empowerment as bishops. They were thereby sharers, Dearden emphasized, in the supreme power of the Church; it was not delegated to them by the pope—it was theirs by virtue of their becoming members of the college of bishops. This supreme power, the cardinal said, "may be exercised in two different ways. To put the matter in theological terms: what we have here is a twofold subject, inadequately distinct, of supreme pastoral power. The first subject (the Pope) is at the same time part or member of the second (the College). Some theologians (such) as Karl Rahner would say that when the Pope exercises supreme power he does so in his role as Head of the Episcopal College."

This theological principle is the blood and breath of episcopal vitality. Professed as an article of faith, it effectively unites today's bishops with St. Peter and his fellow apostles on the theological, spiritual, and psychological levels, delivering to them a sense of vocational uniqueness, divine commission and approbation, that is enormously stabilizing and supportive. This is the soul of what has been described as the "episcopal ideal," that well organized and coherent set of beliefs about the bishopric that still vigorously identifies the office and its holders.

This powerfully functional ideal ties the Church together across history, conferring a mystical aura on the long genealogy of the bishops that affirms their special connection with the apostles. This ideal confirms the bishops as men chosen directly by God "from all eternity," as the Catholic cultural phrase puts it, to lead and govern His Church. The Church enfleshes itself as an institution around the sturdy spine of this religious conviction. Outsiders may debate the authenticity of these claims, but they are largely accepted by Catholics, and they are solemnly perceived by bishops as the source of their temporal authority as well as their eternal responsibilities. This set of beliefs makes bishops special both in time and eternity, pressed by obligations but confident of the divine guidance that is an inseparable aspect of their calling. As noted previously, it would be difficult to identify a comparably effective idealization of office associated with any other leaders or administrators in the contemporary world. This must be kept in mind as we examine more closely the men who are chosen to be bishops.

Although the anecdotal folklore is as rich and thick as a Christmas pudding, relatively little scientific data exist about the American Catholic bishops. The Jesuit editor Thomas Reese completed an informal survey of the bishops in 1983 in which he found that roughly 380 bishops serve in the country's 178 dioceses. In addition to the bishops who head dioceses (ordinaries), there are about 115 assistant bishops (auxiliaries) and some 80 retired prelates. The USCC does not possess a demographic breakdown of the bishops, but

Crux, a religious newsletter, analyzed the 47-member administrative board of the NCBB early in 1985. This group, which runs the conference in between its annual meetings, is composed of the principal officers, committee chairmen, and elected regional representatives, including 2 cardinals, 12 archbishops, 25 bishop ordinaries, and 8 auxiliary bishops. Their ages range from forty-six to seventy-four, with an average of fifty-six years.

Although, as Reese notes, the bishops technically constitute an elite group, "their social origins appear to be rather modest—64 percent of their fathers did not graduate from high school, and only 12 percent graduated from college . . . These findings indicate that there is no clear link between socioeconomic class and higher office in the American Catholic Church as there is in many other organizations."* Reese suggests that working-class roots may explain why the bishops have consistently taken "liberal" positions on economic questions. He also notes that these progressive stands have always echoed those of papal labor encyclicals.

The educational background of the bishops is also instructive in that it reveals how much they are the product of the Catholic educational system. Two thirds of them began their studies in a high school

*This quote and the quotes on the next few pages are from Thomas J. Reese, S. J., "A Survey of the American Bishops," *America,* November 12, 1983.

seminary, and almost half of them attended only seminaries for higher education. Forty-five percent also
attended a nonseminary Catholic college or university
for at least part of their education. About 10 percent
have earned doctorates in nonecclesiastical fields,
while just under a third have master's degrees. Reese's
survey found 10 percent of the prelates with doctorates in theology, and another 10 percent with equivalent degrees in Church law. Another 10 percent have
lesser degrees in the latter ecclesiastical speciality.
Reese observes that most of these degrees were earned
either at the Gregorian University in Rome or at the
Catholic University of America in Washington,
D.C., schools he describes as "ecclesiastical academies
recognized as training grounds for bishops." A third
of the bishops report studying for some time in
Rome; another third report attending the Catholic
University in Washington.

The bishops' work histories prior to their appointments also illustrate the cultural pathway along which
they journeyed to their present positions. Eighty percent of them had worked in diocesan chancery offices,
a quarter of them as chancellor. Half of them report
having had that title or that of vicar-general, assistant
chancellor, or secretary to the bishop. The official
diocesan structure also includes other offices not so
directly tied up with canon law. Just under 10 percent
of Reese's sample reported working in Catholic
Charities, while another 10 percent worked in Catholic education. Twenty percent of the bishops had

served as rectors or administrators in seminaries, and 11 percent had taught previously in these institutions.

While the bishops understand their role as pastoral, only a little over a third of them had worked as pastors before becoming members of the hierarchy. Another third of the bishops reported that they had never been pastors at all. Reese mentions evidence that some who report pastoral experience were "chancery officials sent out to be pastors 'to get the experience' immediately prior to becoming bishops."

It is clear that the American bishops are closely identified with the American Catholic culture, that, with very few exceptions, their educational and work experiences have been within its institutions, and that they have been prepared to be, and indeed function largely as, administrators of the structural aspects of American Catholicism. While there is nothing surprising in this finding, it does underscore the bishops' intimate knowledge of and experience with the institutional aspects of the American Catholic culture, of which they are not only first citizens but quintessential products.

It may be argued that, given their ages, the culture from which the present bishops arose no longer exists. Like their brothers and sisters in other walks of life, these bishops, born primarily between the end of World War I and the end of World War II, grew up in a period in which the American Catholic culture was marked both by great achievement and intense and successful insularity from the rest of American life. A vast enterprise, its energies were harnessed by and through the National Catholic Welfare Conference, the parent organization of the one to which the bishops now belong. This cultural period witnessed a strong public loyalty both to America and to the papacy, well symbolized in the side-by-side display of the American and papal flags in every Catholic school across the country. That cultural epoch emphasized evangelization: personal sanctity, conversion of non-Catholics to the faith, broader impact on and transformation of the host culture of America through education and example flowing from lives shaped by Catholic moral principles.

The Church-dominated culture of that period also expected obedience to its fully detailed regulations and expectations. In short, a demanding, cohesive, sometimes exasperating but often exhilarating culture in which to grow up, the last island of innocence, according to some observers, in the blood-red sea of disillusionment that had risen out of the World War I and the Depression, events that all but destroyed the Protestant progressive religious identification of virtue and prosperity. Catholicism had preserved a tragic sense about life and sin, and instilled this in its believers through its enormous parish and school system. Catholics whose lives were formed by that culture now look upon it with a mixture of feelings, but they recognize its powerful influence on their lives and outlook. Only recently, for example, has a literature of self–observation begun to develop in which the rich

Catholic experience of that time is being explored in novels and plays. The American "Catholic" literature of the period itself was largely defensive and apologetic in tone.

Although that culture was modified by Vatican II —and largely by persons who grew up within its walls—it remains the source of the faith convictions, spiritual ideals, and psychological attitudes of millions of adult Catholics. This culture, tight and well organized, thoroughly imprinted Catholicism on all those who lived within its boundaries. Even those who have left the formal Church acknowledge the enduring impact of growing up in this environment of faith and duty.

Putting aside questions about the post–Vatican II transformation of that culture, it can be said that no persons deliver a better understanding of that culture's discipline and faith than the present American Catholic bishops. Their deeply held beliefs about the Church and its mission, their sense of responsibility for its stewardship, their commitment to its vast enterprises to shape belief and values, their personalities and styles of life—all these derive from the density of their Catholic experience. No men ever marched more truly out of the ideals of the older Catholic culture than these bishops. That they may be engaged in leading that culture into an imaginative reconstruction of itself in no way diminishes the central truth about them: They represent the carefully selected and specially tended harvest of the Catholic culture that reached its high point as a life and belief system unto itself under the supervision of their own episcopal godfathers in the earliest part of this century.

Today's bishops may, in fact, resemble their fore-bears in the hierarchy far more than many contemporary observers, including their critics, realize. While it remains true that a generation of bishops well grounded in the decrees of Vatican II has come into its own and that through implementation of the collegial dictates and spirit of that council they are giving a new shape to American Catholicism, these very men possess many of the personality constructs and basic attitudes of the bishops of a by-gone era. There are constants in the episcopal lineage, and we should not be surprised to discover a family resemblance across the generations. The process of selecting bishops is the oldest executive recruitment program in history. Its techniques of observation, testing, and choice have been refined through hundreds of years of experience. By now Rome understands very well what it desires in a bishop. The process has been reinforced over the centuries by men who pick out other men with characteristics very much like their own. What are the main features of the episcopal personality?

Dr. Frank J. Kobler of Loyola University of Chicago, along with Dr. Mary Sheehan and Dr. James Schroeder, has carried out extensive research on some 125 members of the American hierarchy who volunteered to cooperate, some through filling out psychological questionnaires, some through undergoing intensive two-hour interviews with clinical psychologists. This pioneering work gives us our best understanding of the psychological qualities that are found in the men chosen to enter the hierarchy. Many students of the American bishops feel that Kobler's assessment resonates strongly with their own knowledge and experience of the same subjects.

Kobler finds his sample of bishops highly intelligent, articulate men. "No matter how one measures or evaluates these bishops," he says, "they turn out to be a well adjusted group." Their adjustment, he suggests, is superior to that of the body of priests from which they come and is "highly similar to that of men in comparable positions of power and status. There are a few bishops whose adjustment is marginal or questionable, but their number by any criterion . . . is low." Their psychosexual maturity is achieved, in Kobler's judgment, "at a high price commensurate with their acceptance of celibacy" and is maintained by the effective use of "denial, sublimation, and suppression."[1] These latter psychological terms correspond with traditional spiritual ways of adjusting to celibacy, as, for example, through channeling personal energy into worthy causes and leading controlled and disciplined lives.

The bishops, partly as a result of the effort they put into seeking a well-regulated spiritual ideal, report

[1] Frank J. Kobler, Ph.D., "The American Catholic Bishops: A Psychological Study," Loyola University, Chicago.

good feelings about themselves and their lives. "The central organizing factors in their lives," Kobler observes, "are their jobs as priests and bishops and their church." In other words, the men who are bishops quite effectively build their existences around the ecclesiastical institution, identifying their "calling" with their heavily administrative obligations. They tend to be "highly conservative" in terms of theology and religion and "considerably more liberal" about social issues. This apparently contradictory set of dispositions matches that of earlier twentieth-century bishops and illustrates, across what only appears to be an episcopal generation gap, the consistent good match between the bishops' personalities and the needs and expectations of the institutional church.

The bishops endorse wholeheartedly the institution and its authority; their embrace of liberal social opinions not only reflects their working-class backgrounds but, perhaps more important, their commitment to what the popes teach in their encyclicals on such questions. Their convictions correspond with those of the official Church; indeed, that is one of the career expectations made of them, and it requires underlying personality characteristics that are systematically sought out in potential candidates for the episcopacy. The bishops are not and never will be rebels against the pope or Church authority. They may explore the full limits of their newly emphasized collegiality, but they perceive this as authority and responsibility that comes to them from the Church itself and hence as in harmony with their dedication. They may also enter into their new opportunities as members of a national conference, but again this is seen as a commission that comes from the Church itself through official conciliar decrees.

Their identification with the ecclesiastical institution is further enhanced by their orientation toward achievement. Kobler identifies this as his most consistent finding in the population he studied. "The sense of duty," in Kobler's analysis, "is paramount in the bishop's life. They operate out of a 'must' context. On the other hand, they avoid, neglect, obscure, and deny the feeling aspects of life." In other words, like many professionals, the bishops have strong obsessive-compulsive tendencies, and they are not psychologically minded in their approach to life. They lead busy lives, in which there are demands on their time around the clock. They like it that way, just as they enjoy the administrative work that they do. Although extremely bright, the bishops are not, with few exceptions, intellectuals interested in the world of ideas. As Kobler notes, these dutiful men "see life in relation to divine responsibilities . . . The obligations and responsibilities arising from their work are central to their thoughts. Duty, work, achievement, accomplishment keep recurring in what they say and think."

The bishops are not, with few exceptions, creative persons. Everything about their personalities orients them toward resolving rather than relishing ambiguity. They are expected to administer a Church that does not change easily or quickly in any way, and their neutrality with respect to creativity serves them and the institutional Church quite well. A truly creative person would be called upon to make extraordinary, perhaps impossibly difficult, adjustments to meet the behavioral and attitudinal expectations made on bishops. They are fundamentally men of the institution, whose psychological qualities of dutifulness and hard work contribute enormously to the Church's stability and to their sense of divine approbation.

The bishops make their institutional commitment on the basis of their religious faith. They believe in the Church and in the authority given to it by Jesus Christ. Their beliefs may be orthodox and conventional, but they are firmly held and, as such, contribute not only to their own adjustment but to the strength of the Church as a teaching force. The bishops firmly believe in the divine ordering of the Catholic Church. As part of that they accept their own selection as bishops as a providential event; they may feel unworthy, the recipients of great gifts from God, but they are also strongly convinced that they have been chosen to be bishops from all eternity. This is powerfully enhancing to their self-esteem and reinforces their commitment to the tasks given to them in a highly effective manner.

They have power from God, which they distinguish from any personal power of their own. It is fascinating to observe how strongly an individual may be affected by being named a bishop. For many prelates, this experience is the central one of their lives. For some its impact is so great, psychologically and spiritually, that it causes a crisis for them. They feel, through being chosen, that they are removed, in a real sense, from the ordinary plane of life and placed on a higher one. They can accept this because, as they see it, their being chosen is a function of divine power and plan rather than of any human effort on their part. They can discount any elements of personal ambition under the aura of their calling and ordination into the extraordinary fraternity of the episcopacy. They tend to deny having any personal power, and although they describe a certain uneasiness about the power they see as granted to them from on high, they accept it, and feel transformed by it.

These are potent elements of what has been referred to as the "episcopal ideal." The nature of the episcopal office, as it has been transmitted through the teaching of the Catholic Church across the centuries, places a man in a unique and extremely responsible relationship to Jesus Christ. He perceives himself as chosen as much as St. Peter to preserve and expand Christ's Church. This core belief, supported by tradition and invested with extraordinary rights, distinctive authority, and a variety of public duties and privileges, reinforces the personality characteristics and faith commitments of the men who are selected for the episcopacy. The abiding perennial strength and appeal of this office as a mark of preferment and a sign of spiritual destiny provide a man with a new and strongly positive concept of himself. He feels taken out of time and linked with the eternally determined line of apostolic succession. It is little wonder that Kobler finds bishops much more oriented toward the past and the future than toward the present. Their office places them in a perspective that is shared by few others. They see the Church as always transcending the moment as they faithfully help to keep it balanced and orthodox as it moves ever forward.

As noted, the bishops often construe their power as something external to themselves, something given to them as a gift and an obligation by God. "This impersonality of power," Kobler observes, "with its divine origin sets bishops apart from other power holders in the modern world. It is akin to the power held by Alexander and Augustus, a pharaoh, or a medieval king in whom it was thought to be divine in origin, and therefore unassailable and unimpugnable by man." The surrounding Catholic culture also views a bishop's power along these lines. As Kobler explains, "The bishop defends his power and the Church which provides this power. Power so provided and defended tends toward conservation and toward authoritarianism . . . The bishop sustains this power and the acts that flow from it, be they desirable or undesirable in the eyes of others, by the unequivocal reference to the source of his power." Bishops tend, therefore, to feel secure about their exercise of power, and, as Kobler observes, "it is difficult to find a bishop who feels guilty for anything he has done . . . The fact that the bishop is a good man leading a good life tends to reinforce this." Such power reassures, and absolute power of this kind reassures absolutely.

The American Catholic bishops are therefore men of stability, high morale, and devotion to their duty to the Church around which their lives are built. They are especially loyal to the pope, their brother bishop, with whom they share in God's own delegation of power. The approval of the pope, as the head of the college of bishops, is extremely significant to them, for he embodies the authoritative Church that rises like a cathedral in a town square at the very center of their lives. Their perception of their selection allows them to look away from questions of personal ambition, even though these are obviously real issues at times, because of the overwhelming mandate of their being chosen to serve an institution greater than themselves. They are being obedient by accepting roles of authority and power. They also enjoy administrative work and, indeed, would be uncomfortable if called on to function otherwise. Tempermentally, they are ideally suited to the routine of paperwork, meetings, and consultations that constitute their lives. That disposes them well to the endless bureacratic aspects of their existences both as diocesan administrators and members of a national conference. Intelligent and able, they feel great confidence about their own vocations of service, especially because the episcopal ideal guarantees divine guidance for their work.

This makes the American Catholic bishops a formidable group, perhaps a good deal like the bishops of previous generations, who, from historical records, seem to have possessed very similar personality traits. That today's bishops are committed to the moderate changes of Vatican II does not make them mavericks or excessively innovative; they perceive their carrying out of this program as their duty, just as their episcopal predecessors viewed carrying out the teachings of Vatican I as their solemn obligation. What binds the generations of American Catholic bishops together is their institutional traditionalism, their profound loyalty to the Church, their belief in its teachings, and their readiness to work unstintingly on its behalf.

Such a cadre of religious leaders represents the interests of the Church as an institution very well and is able to make many sacrifices—and sustain much criticism—in the course of carrying out its obligations. The process of selection works very smoothly in finding men who meet the requirements for being a bishop. The bishops, even if they represent different regions and, at times, even different approaches to the implementation of policy, are more alike than different. They constitute a strong, enduring force, whose capacity for work, survival, and the pursuit of the Church's interests and teachings will not easily be frustrated or turned aside. The American bishops and the institutional Church they lead constitute a remarkably good fit. One would be foolish to underestimate or misinterpret their strength of intellect, character, or orthodox institutional commitment.

THREE

A CASE HISTORY: THE DEVELOPMENT OF THE PASTORAL LETTER ON THE ECONOMY

Fᴇʙʀᴜᴀʀʏ 1984. The pastoral letter on the economy had its origins at the same gathering of bishops in Washington, D.C., in November 1980, that voted to explore Catholic teaching on war and peace. Proposed by then forty-five-year-old Peter A. Rosazza, auxiliary bishop of Hartford, Connecticut, who became a member of the committee chosen to prepare it, the document was originally viewed as complementary to a largely theoretical paper that the prelates had just issued on Communism. In the aftershocks of the nuclear pastoral issued in May 1983, however, the unseen document quickly became the subject of intense and ambivalent anticipation and debate well beyond the borders of American Catholicism.

In addition to the negative reactions from business magazines and the apprehension of government officials, as well as the speculation about the bishops' political motivations in authoring such a letter, some critics wondered if the bishops had adequately considered their own position in a church that reportedly possesses great wealth, some of which is earning a pleasant return in the capital markets, and, while you're at it, ask the pope about the Vatican Bank and its troubles. Did the bishops understand the sensitivity of discussing money, a subject that, now that sex and death had become table topics, bore the full weight of society's last taboo? "Everybody was willing to talk about nuclear war," one skeptical Washington Catholic pastor notes, "but the bishops won't find people that way when it comes to their own pocketbooks."

One must travel to Milwaukee, a city gripped by the upheaval caused by the nation's difficult adjustment to an information age, to find a gritty microcosm containing all the elements of the national economic experience that had raised the pastoral concern of the bishops. The experiences in this city are similar to those that face bishops in all parts of the country.

The old Route 41 up along Lake Michigan from Chicago is still remembered on old-fashioned signs shaped like sheriff's badges but, as a symbol of the era of change, has been rechristened as 94 West on stylized markers colored like the flag. The highway is lined with the abandoned enterprises of another time, just as the outskirts of the city itself are filled with the broken-windowed factories whose whistles once summoned thousands of industrial workers to their shifts. The archbishop of Milwaukee, Rembert G. Weakland, had already begun his work as chairman of the committee preparing the pastoral "Catholic Social Teaching and the American Economy" when first visited early in 1984.

His office, in a spread of buildings that once served as a high school seminary, is as sparely and plainly furnished as the cell of his original calling as a Benedictine monk. The morning light carries a Third World mood, as well as a hint about his own background and sympathies, as it strikes the framed words that hang above his desk. They are those of Archbishop Oscar Romero, slain while offering Mass in his Salvadoran cathedral three years before: "The cry of liberation of these people is a clamor that ascends to God nothing nor no one can stop."

Weakland touches a finger to the bridge of his glasses, sips a mug of Brim, speaks reflectively. "In these pastoral letters the bishops are not writing for political reasons. If we were, we would hardly have taken the positions that we have in defense of human life all across the board. We end up, after all, with right-wing Republicans in our stand against abortion, and with the left wing of the liberal Democrats when we condemn capital punishment. The bishops aren't staking out political territory; we want to begin serious discussions from a moral viewpoint on the major issues of our times."

The archbishop recognizes that not all believers will necessarily agree with the positions taken by the bishops. "We understand that there has to be a continuing discussion, that's why we welcome the Catholic members of the business community who want to join the dialogue on the economy. It's their obligation to take this seriously, to listen to as many voices, especially of the poor, as the bishops have."

Weakland is something of an exception among the bishops, for he is a creative person, a trained musician who once wrote liner notes for *Pro Musica Antiqua* and who served for ten years as head, or abbot primate, of the worldwide Benedictine order, but he is clearly an intellectual leader in that first generation of U.S. Catholic bishops who were formed by and imbued with the spirit of Vatican Council II.

"The business community should not be considered the whipping boy in this letter," Weakland says softly, gazing toward Lake Michigan beyond the windows of his office. "It is unfair that they be that. We have a long tradition of social teaching and a succession of papal encyclicals on labor going back to the last century." The archbishop purses his lips, recalls the era in which the American Catholic Church vigorously supported the labor movement through its forceful teaching of the papal labor encyclicals. "There's nothing new," Weakland says evenly, "in our asking what this tradition of concern has to say about our American economy, especially at this time, when it is going through such a massive transformation.

"The labor encyclicals of Popes Leo XIII [*Rerum Novarum*, 1891] and Pius XI [*Quadragesimo Anno*, 1931] were very significant when labor questions were on the front burner in this country," Weakland continues, "but they disappeared as Catholics succeeded and moved into the professions, the middle class, and the suburbs." The proposed pastoral, he explains, will draw heavily on encyclicals of John XXIII, Paul VI, and John Paul II that are still not as well known as those of earlier popes.

Realizing that they could not examine the American economy solely from a theoretical viewpoint, Weakland and his fellow bishops decided to treat it "as it is found phenomenologically in this country, and, secondarily, as it affects the rest of the world." His collaborators include seventy-two-year-old Atlanta Archbishop Thomas A. Donnellan, a former New Yorker who began his Church career under the financially conservative tutelage of the late Francis Cardinal Spellman. Also working with Weakland is seventy-three-year-old George H. Speltz, who holds a graduate degree in economics and serves as bishop of St. Cloud, Minnesota, a heavily Catholic area with a liberal Democratic tradition. Besides Bishop Rosazza, who not only works with the poor in Waterbury, Connecticut, but conducts regular dialogues with business executives, there is also William K. Weigand, forty-six, who served as a pastor in Colombia, South America, for ten years. Now, as bishop of Salt Lake City, Utah, he lives in simple quarters in the poorest section of that city.

These bishops are in turn served by the Washington-based staff of the USCC, headed by Father J. Bryan Hehir, who also worked prominently on the peace pastoral, and including Monsignor George Higgins, a veteran labor specialist, and Mr. Ronald P. Krietmeyer, director of the USCC's office of domestic social development. Working closely with them are many consultants, including the economist Charles Wilber of the University of Notre Dame and Donald Warwick of Harvard's International Development Department. Also assisting are two economist members of religious orders, the Dominican sister Margaret Ann Cahill and the Jesuit priest Michael Lavelle. When critics suggest the existence of a liberal bias against business among these counselors, the bishops reply that they are listening, through an extensive consultation network, to a wide variety of opinions in a collegial process that strives to develop the right questions rather than to provide the ultimate answers.

Archbishop Weakland hefts a volume of papal encyclicals as an absorbed orchestra conductor would a familiar score. As he speaks, one overhears a clear prophecy of the thrust of the document in preparation. "We have chosen four areas. The first is employment generation. There is a case to be made from

Catholic social teaching for making job creation a real national priority. We also want to discuss the question of adequate income for the poor and disadvantaged. Church teaching about human dignity demands that we address this both in terms of policy and implementation."

Weakland walks across the office to the windows that face northward toward downtown Milwaukee. "We also," he continues, "wanted one area outside the United States, something that could be read in the Third World, like that of U.S. trade with developing countries." He opens the book. "Pope John XXIII began to shift our reference point from the common good of individual nations to the common good of the universe." Weakland's tone underscores this concept, which challenges competitive American businessmen to think of the good of others instead of just their own bottom line as they make economic policy decisions, as one of the keys to the forthcoming pastoral. "That is *central* . . ."

He flips to another page. "Our last area is economic planning and policy. Not so much *what* but *who* is involved in economic planning. If you look at it closely, you recognize that we have a planned economy. But it's just the government that does the planning. One of the most challenging statements in John Paul II's *Laborem Exercens* (1981) is that the dignity of the workers demands that they have a part in the decisions that affect their lives." His emphasis makes it obvious that the current pope's thinking, which some critics label as socialistic in its claims that workers have a right to share not only in the business profits but in its means of production as well, will emerge as a major theme of the letter in preparation. The archbishop smiles as he looks toward the city. "Big business is very concerned about what we say in this area."

In a private room on the second floor in the brick fastness of Milwaukee's University Club, retired Admiral Elmo R. Zumwalt, Jr., formerly chairman of the Joint Chiefs of Staff, and now chairman of American Medical Buildings, Inc., inspects, from beneath sprigged brows, three heads of local companies gathered to discuss the bishops' letter and its principal architect, their city's archbishop.

"Regarding the economy, the bishops may kill the goose that lays the golden eggs," Zumwalt declares in a voice deep and sharp enough to shout orders into a hurricane. "They grossly oversimplified the issues in their letter on war and peace." He smiles as he snaps open the flag of his napkin. "I hope they do better this time."

At the far end of the table, William Brady, chairman of an adhesive manufacturing concern, sixtyish, sandy hair above an outdoorsman's face, leans forward. "I'm a convert to Catholicism but may I say that the Catholic Church has a nonrecord—I won't even say it's dismal—of competence in the discipline of economics?"

Leon T. Kendall, chairman of the Mortgage Guaranty Insurance Corporation, is also a Catholic. A

balding man in his forties, Kendall projects careful-
ness, thoughtfulness; he did not choose his expensive
dark suit impulsively. "These bishops," he says
calmly, "will advocate social planning that doesn't
work. France is our best current example. You must
permit, you cannot order, choice. Otherwise, you end
up with the failures of Soviet Russia, where they built
roads and bridges where no towns ever grew." He
pauses, clears his throat. "My position is that I will
read their letter respectfully, view its source, understand its heritage, and will then go about my business."

William Law, president of the Cudahy Tanning
Company, is a non-Catholic student both of economy
and of papal statements on capital and labor. His
boyish face is aged like fine paneling. "It may be
implicit in the bishops' approach," he observes dryly,
"that the actions of businessmen are arbitrary. The
businessman cannot be arbitrary. If he pays above the
market, *ceteris paribus,* he is expelled. He is not a
captain, he is a pilot. The consumer is the captain."

Zumwalt glances at his outsize Navy watch. "The
bishops seek to appeal to the good in man. It makes
them unrealistic, as when they called for an uncondi-
tional nuclear freeze, something that would increase
the dangers of war. They fail to see that what works
most efficiently is that which flows from greed."

"I'm afraid," Brady says slowly, "the bishops don't
understand that real wealth comes from productivity."

"They don't understand capital formation," Law

interjects, "and if they perceive wealth, they think it should be distributed. But it is of much greater value to everybody to increase it. Unfortunately," he sighs, " 'the rich' has a pejorative connotation. We would appreciate them better if, instead, we called them 'the producers.' "

"I don't go to Mass," Brady counters, "to get a social message from the priest." Laughter erupts as he continues, "I go there to be pulled up short."

"The bishops' capacity to impact men in business is slight," Kendall says, "but they can have a real impact on those passing through their Catholic schools."

"The pope has infiltrated me from below," Zumwalt says good-naturedly. "I'm not Catholic, but I have four Catholic grandchildren. They may learn to despise the system I'm a part of."

"When the bishops do this kind of thing they spend their credibility," Brady says, "and some measure of their authority in transcendent realms."

"I think," Kendall says, "that Archbishop Weakland's monastic background affects his view of the economic system. In a monastic community, you have a vow of poverty. Reasonable harmony comes out of the system; somebody cooks, somebody sews, everybody has something to do. Now that's the system that Weakland selected and grew up in. That's socialism. It doesn't train you to see the virtues of the market system."

As Kendall describes the dynamic nature of the

American economic system and its dependence on free choices at every level, one realizes that these men are true believers in capitalism, which they feel was blessed by the Catholic Church when, in the seventeenth century, it removed the ban on usury that it had gradually modified over the previous five centuries. Following Aristotle, the Catholic Church had previously taught that it was intrinsically evil to charge interest for the use of money, which, unlike animals or plants, was considered "barren" and incapable of fruitful self-reproduction. The changing perception and nature of money—that it was anything but infertile in then developing commerce—contributed, according to Dr. John T. Noonan of the University of California at Berkeley, along with increasingly subtle philosophical analyses and a better understanding of the experience of Christian bankers, to the development of liberalized Church teaching.

"It is an oversimplification," Noonan warns, "to think, as some have, that capitalism only prospered under Protestant reformers. These factors were at work for a long time and, in fact, the first use of the word 'capital' was in the city states of Florence." The Milwaukee businessmen view themselves as inheritors of a long, pragmatic yet moral tradition that bases its operation on the principle, accepted by St. Thomas Aquinas, that the conditions of supply and demand in an open market determine a "just price" and, as a common estimate of value, exclude exploitation.

A few days later, ninety miles south along the lake,

looking down from another private luncheon club through the pale noontime light at the sparkling quadrants of Chicago, Walter E. Auch, chairman and chief executive officer of the Chicago Board Options Exchange, speaks as a bittersweet Everyman for Catholic businessmen uneasy about the pastoral letter in progress. "This won't be a document presented by the bishops but a document presented by the media. I have grave concern for its impact on the system. And equally grave concern for its impact on the Church and its priorities." He sips coffee but will not be comforted. "It makes me feel an estrangement from the Church as a community. They set out to criticize me and my life without asking me to look at it and see what we can do about it. What I've learned"— he locks his eyes on those of his luncheon companions —"is that the bishops' style is to look for me when they want donations, but *not* to seek my counsel." He taps the table impatiently. "I don't want them to put me in a position where I feel driven away from a faith I've worked harder at than my business."

"It's very sad," says Donna Ruddofsky, "what this is doing to families, to people who were in the middle class, like us, and have dropped out of it." She gazes out of her kitchen window at West Allis, a south Milwaukee suburb that holds a mood of remembered activity as a museum does that of another time. "People have lost homes, marriages, and lots of them are so ashamed that they won't even talk about it." West

the economy. "The organizations arrayed against them—the Business Round Table, the magazines, people like William Buckley—they're so powerful . . ." Unspoken longing fills the sudden interval of quiet. A lawnmower drones rhythmically somewhere in the otherwise hushed neighborhood. Donna Ruddofsky folds her hands in front of her. "Personally, I feel it's about time the bishops got into this. The clergy are generally the best group to know what's going on in the heart of people, and the bishops may be the only ones who can give some depth of perception of how people are being devastated. The bishops have to speak because otherwise society doesn't want to look at this kind of human suffering."

Oklahoma Avenue runs as smooth as a ruler's edge through Milwaukee's south side, past rows of candy-box homes still owned, for the most part, by employees who could walk to work in the factories that crowd the farther stretches of the broad street. Kenneth A. Germanson, as slim and leathery in his late fifties as an old ballplayer-turned-scout, is director of communications and legislation for the Allied Industrial Workers of America. A Proustian note of boom times remembered invades his voice as he speaks of his own union's loss of ninety-one plants and roughly one third of its membership in the last five years.

His companion, Earl Lepp, silver-haired and robust-looking enough to be a bishop himself, is, in fact, secretary-treasurer of the Milwaukee County Labor

Council. He recites a mournful litany of the closed factories that now crowd the route. "Perfex is for sale, and Caterpillar there will close next year. That'll be another five hundred jobs lost. The Patrick Cudahy meat company is going out of business, and that's about a thousand more jobs we'll lose. We project that by 1985, southeast Wisconsin will be down over seventy-two thousand manufacturing jobs from the 1979 levels." The car pulls up at Ye Old Dinner Bell, a small restaurant, once noisy every noontime with customers from the nearby plants. From its front steps one sees tractors plowing up the employee parking lot of the now shuttered railway equipment plant of the Rexnord Corporation.

The mood of the meal is that of a luncheon of old, he's-dead, what-can-you-say-now companions after a friend's funeral on a sunny morning. The union leaders see America's middle class being driven, as inevitably as cattle in a round-up, into the pen of poverty. Labor feels suddenly alone. "You can't count on any political party," Lepp says, adding that the unions are not sure just what their onetime staunch supporter, the Catholic Church, will do to help.

"We've had an arms-length relationship for a generation now," he continues, explaining the conflicts that labor experienced in trying to organize the workers in many Catholic schools and hospitals. It remains a cracked and stinging tooth in labor's mouth, which it cannot leave alone. "Archbishop Weakland here in Milwaukee has let us organize in the institutions under his control, but it hasn't always been that way. Still, we welcome the bishops getting into this. I just hope, after the long vacuum in our relationship, that it won't be too little and too late. Our members are saying, Where have they been all this time?"

Germanson cites Catholic Church support for Cesar Chavez and the farm workers, as well as the prominent roles played by bishops in recent years in securing union gains in the J.P. Stevens and the Farah workers' strike, as well as in seeking worker ownership for Youngstown, Ohio's, closing steel plants. "Why wouldn't the bishops play a role in this?" Lepp asks. "They have to recognize how the middle class is suffering, how the poor are dropping out completely. They *must* do something. We have to work together in a more positive way, especially for the next generation. The real crunch is coming for young people who will be just hitting their stride at the turn of the century. We need the bishops' help *now*."

West Milwaukee's Vliet Street cuts through an aldermanic ward that is a torn and soiled map of a half century of urban change. Now worn-looking, as if the Depression, the war, and the sixties had finally broken them, the neighborhoods are black and poor, and the unemployment rate is 44 percent. Housed in a storefront in the 2500 block is Weatherization and Retrofit Milwaukee (WARM), a cooperative, following the model of Wisconsin dairy farmers, established in 1982 by a score of jobless young black men.

"We were unemployed," one of them says.

"*Very* unemployed," a companion corrects amid a shower of laughter.

"We started with nothing but our own assets," says Andrew White, a husky young man in a blue T-shirt, "and it's still a struggle. We've had help from the Congress for Working America, a national organization that supports co-ops"—he nods toward two of its staff who are visiting—"and we've been able to do seventy thousand dollars' worth of business."

"I feel really good about myself," the quill-bearded vice-president, Clyde Adams, interjects in a circle of nodding heads. "The thing is we do the input, and we own the output. It's a feeling that you're controlling your own destiny."

The city's synagogues and churches helped them establish credit with their suppliers. Grants totaling $25,000 from religious groups enabled them to purchase bookkeeping equipment and the necessary transportation. "Our needs are so small," one of the group explains, "that banks and government agencies can't even *see* us. We're invisible, so the churches are crucial to our survival."

John Gardner, a burly young white man from the national organization, which supports cooperatives in New York, Michigan, and Rhode Island, as well as three others in Milwaukee, joins the discussion. "Historically, the religious institutions have been the first, and sometimes the only ones, to defend folks with no other defense. Today we have a systematic onslaught on the dignity of those seeking work. The synagogues and churches are the ones who *can* turn it around. And the bishops' letter—I'd say right now it's our *only* hope . . ."

"Yes," adds Brian Yamel, a WARM board member, who speaks softly, reflectively. "To me the bishops' support is very important. The government sees the problem but doesn't want to do anything about it. What the bishops have been doing is waking people up."

A few blocks north of the University Club, two former Catholic priests, Jack Murtagh and Pat Flood, work together at the Greater Milwaukee Conference on Religion and Urban Affairs, sponsored by fourteen local religious groups to promote an ongoing dialogue between business and religious leaders on the ethical dimensions of such issues as closing plants without warning. Their faces are as Irish as those of two former citizens of Milwaukee, Spencer Tracy and Pat O'Brien.

Murtagh sighs, sweeps his hands through the air as he once did saying Mass. "The hierarchy of business is very rigid. And the higher they get, the more careful they are. They wonder what the boss thinks of everything they do. How do they bring a faith dimension to the bottom line? It's difficult because they take their work environment as a given, as something beyond questioning from the viewpoint of values."

Flood retrieves some papers left over from a just-ended meeting as he speaks. "Most businessmen want to deal with an opposite number; the chief executives all want to deal directly with Archbishop Weakland. And what businessmen mostly want to do is educate religious leaders to their view of things."

They seem more weary pastors than angry revolutionaries as Murtagh speaks. "The civic religion of America says that we should support the economic system. Businessmen want religion to form individuals who then enter a world where the churches should stay out. They'd like bishops to bless the economy, the way they used to bless battleships. But we're in such a period of transition, and it is affecting so many people, and the churches are the only institutions strong enough to provide the forum for an in-depth examination of the moral issues involved. I think that's what Archbishop Weakland personifies on the national level."

You can buy the *Business Journal* from a vending box in front of St. John's Cathedral rectory, where Archbishop Weakland lives in a modest suite of rooms made smaller by crowded tiers of books and a Mason and Hamlin baby grand. Weakland, wearing a red and black checked jacket over his open-collared clerical shirt, knew hard times during his Depression era childhood in Patton, Pennsylvania. The small family-operated hotel burned in 1931, and his father died the next year, leaving his schoolteacher mother to raise six children on her own.

A theme runs through his recollections of growing up, resolving his conflict about becoming a musician or a priest—"I felt I couldn't spend my life entertaining, and I went without looking back"—and his studying at New York's Juilliard School of Music and at Columbia University in the early fifties before he became, at forty, an abbot primate, and, at fifty, an archbishop. From his first parish priest to memorable professors to Monsignor James O'Reilly, who gave him a "novitiate in reality" when he lived under him in New York City's St. Malachy's Church, he speaks of people who "have been good to me, very good to me."

He feels that becoming head of the international Benedictine order in 1967 prepared him well for his present task of examining an American economy as intertwined as the letters of an illuminated manuscript. "It was an excellent job," he says, again in the tones of a man who has discovered hospitality in unlikely places. "I spent half my time traveling, visiting five hundred and fifty monasteries of men and women in every corner of the globe. I traveled extensively behind the Iron Curtain every other year. I came to know the present pope well when he was archbishop of Cracow." The late Pope Paul VI, whom Weakland describes as "a strong supporter of mine," named him archbishop of Milwaukee in 1977.

Despite the anticipatory criticism of his committee's work, he seems serene. "Yes, I am," he responds with an easy laugh. "I think, when I get down to it, that I know as much as any of them about the world.

My job as abbot primate was to deal with cultural pluralism on a worldwide scale. I had to keep people talking to each other." He folds his arms, speaks like a man who trusts his own instincts. "That's a big part of the way the American bishops deal with issues. They want to keep people talking, get as many capable people involved in major issues like war and peace as possible. That process of dialogue is an integral part of who we are. And Americans are good at it. It's that kind of process that we are using to develop our letter on the economy."

That process has led Weakland and his colleagues through dozens of consultations with a wide range of experts: economists, including former presidential economic advisers Charles Schultze and Herbert Stein; businessmen, including several executives from General Motors; academics; theologians; labor leaders, such as Thomas Donahue, secretary-treasurer of the AFL-CIO; and leaders of other religions. They have also received written comments from other interested people and plan to have extensive discussions of their drafts as they point to a November 1985 goal for the completion of the document.

Weakland rises and stands by the piano, on which rests a sheaf of Chopin's music. He does seem at peace, not fully immune to criticism but free of concern about its consequences for his career, as if he had thought that all out long ago, when he decided to become a monk instead of a musician. "There is no question," he says, "that the Church must also examine itself and its practices as an economic actor with the same kind of responsibilities as any kind of big business. We presuppose the concern and the goodwill of the business community toward the poor and the underprivileged. Its members are just as concerned as we are about the society in which we live. That's why we're glad to have them participate in a real exchange about the ethical problems in the economy. That's what the process is all about, getting people to think about their lives and work in terms of the Gospel."

He straightens the music score as he continues, "We are really raising the same questions that Pope John Paul II has, particularly in his talks in such countries as Mexico, Korea, Brazil, and Haiti. It is difficult for every Catholic to take a hard look at these problems. It may be disturbing at times, but that is, as we see it, what our beliefs ask us to do. We realize that the questions are so large that no single component of the economy has all the answers. And we have to think in international, global terms. The Church is already a multinational moral force, and so it is already in place to examine and speak about the moral implications of economic issues." He raises his hand, as if fending off an objection. "If the Church in the past has neglected to say much about productivity, and should do so now, it still doesn't take away its need to talk about a more equitable distribution of wealth."

He lingers a moment next to the piano, which he often plays before dinner in the evening. "The accusation that monasticism breeds socialism," he says softly, "is interesting when you remember that the roots of Western civilization came out of that monastic experiment. Our concern for the land, for people, for our resources, all of that. Monasticism provided a basis for Western culture. It has deep biblical roots." He smiles. "That sounds like a good challenge for any society.

"Religious leaders," Archbishop Weakland says, "have a tough time knowing at what moment they should be prophetic and challenging, and at what time they should be healing and comforting. Keeping these in balance is exactly what bishops are called to do."

November 1984. Russ Chandler, religion writer for the Los Angeles *Times,* adjusts the microphone slightly. Archbishop Rembert Weakland looks down expectantly from the dais at the far end of the Congressional Room of the Capital Hilton in Washington, D.C. The Milwaukee prelate has just introduced the first draft of the American Catholic bishops' proposed letter on the economy and, under chandeliers glistening like icicles in the television lights, he is answering questions from some of the 450 journalists accredited to cover the bishops' meeting.

"Which parts of the letter," Chandler asks as the snap and slide of cameras picks up again, "are most at variance with the Reagan administration?"

Weakland smiles. "That has not been analyzed," he responds to a rising chuckle, "but the bishops think they will find out soon enough about it."

Find out they do as a torrent of reaction to the 112-page draft document sweeps across the headlines and newscasts of the country. Illinois Republican Representative Henry Hyde, a Catholic who identifies strongly with the bishops' position on abortion, decries their present efforts. "The bishops have been swept away by the prophet motive—that's P-R-O-P-H-E-T." Michael Novak, the Catholic philosopher who had already collaborated with former Treasury Secretary William Simon and a self-selected group of lay dissenters on a paper issued the previous week as a preemptive strike on the as yet unseen contents of the episcopal document, immediately writes an op-ed piece for the Washington *Post* criticizing it as "whiney and ungenerous." He accuses the bishops of wanting to give the federal government "new and sweeping powers" to assign wages, raise the minimum wage, limit personal income and family wealth, and usurp local laws in setting welfare standards.

Other commentators, such as Charles Corddry, normally achingly judicious on Public Television's *Washington Week in Review,* snort about the bishops' bad timing and bad judgment. While some financial writers, including Leonard Silk of the New York *Times,* with a hint of admiration for the bishops, reflect calmly on the need for a moral appraisal of the American economic system, the reviews match the previews that had appeared in business magazines months earlier. Had the draft document been a play, these anticipatory reviews, some bittersweet, some just bitter about the bishops getting in over their heads, would have closed it on the road.

One thing is clear: The American Catholic bishops, unlike their Episcopalian opposite numbers, whose October 1984 pastoral letter on religion and politics disappeared almost without a trace, are not being ignored. Have they, some wonder, become a collective St. George, challenging the dragon of American complacency, whose tail, as John Cheever once wrote, can be heard stirring the leaves on the lush green lawns of the nation's suburban dreamworld?

January 1985. Half a fierce winter later, Archbishop Weakland smiles again as he seats himself at a small round conference table in his office. Yes, he nods, the reactions have been coming in from all over the country, and his committee is preparing to revise its initial draft for further discussion by the bishops in June 1985. "One of the things I've learned," he says in his soft, melodic voice, "is that if something *can* be misunderstood, it *will* be misunderstood." He grins and settles in his chair as I ask about the charges that the bishops want to hand vast powers of societal intervention over to the government.

Weakland nods thoughtfully; he prefers to focus on issues rather than individual criticisms of the bishops' efforts. Michael Novak's Washington *Post* column that made these claims has already been branded by *Commonweal,* among others, as a deliberate distortion of the bishops' position. "The idea," Weakland says, "that the bishops cited five items as defects in the system and were going to ask the government to intervene in each is not borne out by reading the document. We only speak of the federal government's role in overhauling the welfare system." He pauses, a man who will let the bishops' work speak for itself. "When we say that the disparity between the rich and the poor is morally unacceptable, we are not saying, 'Let's make all the rich people poor.' That kind of interpretation does an injustice to the document."

The archbishop speaks gently but does not smile as he continues, "The big distortions of the draft document lie in the accusation that we are advocating big government, statism of some kind, and, second, that we are advocating a kind of dependent welfarism. These notions are easy to refute. We basically offer two arguments. The first concerns the fundamental dignity of the human person, and the second argues that this can only be achieved through participation in the economy. When we say that dignity is achieved through participation in the economy, we are not advocating a welfare state but, in fact, are urging that it be avoided."

The archbishop leans back. Spread out on the desk behind him lies evidence of his own financial concerns and of his acquaintance with ledger sheets and payrolls, a sample poster for the forthcoming archdiocesan stewardship drive. What, I ask him, are the sources of this seemingly conscious distortion of the pastoral-in-the-making? "I think some of these superficial but harsh criticisms derive from some people's keen political sense that this would be a good way to destroy this document in the eyes of others. Many people attacked this draft before they even read it."

Weakland leans on the edge of the table, as intent as a chess player in his concentration. "There are many groups of Catholic business executives, however, who have been very interested in contributing positively to the dialogue that is necessary for the development of this letter. I have had opportunities to meet with several of these groups in different parts of the country. I find them very concerned about some of the major issues, such as poverty and unemployment, that some critics want to sweep under the rug. As to our document, these executives have no difficulty with the biblical theology and they speak of needing to 'think more in these terms.' Talking to these men, I get a very strong sense of their interest and their desire to be constructive in their comments and suggestions.

"These men do hold hands, however, in their conviction that they should do more and the government less in resolving economic problems. A liberatarian philosophy is really taking root in the business community. Why they think that the private sector should be better than the government is beyond me, but they feel strongly about this. For them, as for most American business interests, the great freedom for the free-enterprise system is freedom from government supervision."

He is puzzled at the firmness of their commitment

to this fundamental article of their economic credo. "This attitude seems second nature to them. How, I wonder, are they going to compete with Japan, a country that puts so much effort and capital into assisting industry? These businessmen are deathly afraid of planning as it is found in Japan. Japan is the greatest threat to the U.S. because they have taken our system and gone it one better. American businessmen are very pragmatic in their desire to keep the government out—they are really very anti-Congress—and make all the decisions themselves. In their thinking, we are really witnessing a return to the pre-Rooseveltian era." He smiles wryly. "Economists will tell you that the freest period for business was during the Hoover administration.

"On the other hand, they are inconsistent because they strongly support the defense budget and, therefore, the *strongest* government." Weakland speaks like a man intrigued by the design of the intellectual puzzle as he fits a last segment of insight into it. "They see that they cannot operate in a free world economy without their security strongly guaranteed. If you want to compete, you cannot let the Russians take over too much prime territory. Many businessmen support the defense budget not out of fear of military threat but out of a fear of economic threat. They see the world divided into two main economic spheres, with a big in-between segment. They are strongly anti-Communist from an economic point of view."

Winter is sewing a frosty shroud around the buildings that contain not only Weakland's office but those of several other diocesan services and educational facilities as well. The former seminary is a formidable symbol of the Church that lived so successfully within its own walled kingdom before Vatican II. Dedicated just three years before that council began, its plans betrayed no imaginative intuitions about the future. It held a 500-desk study hall that was supervised by priest-prefects in conning towerlike stations. The original rector, reflecting the spirit of the times, specified that the swimming pool be built a few lengths short of Olympic size so that it would be easy to turn away outsiders seeking to use it for practice. The same commitment to isolation from the world inspired the decision not to build restrooms near the auditorium theater. These seem feeble ghosts who can no longer find a haunt in the diocesan headquarters of an archbishop so profoundly involved with the once forbidden world.

"These business leaders," Weakland continues, straightening the green baize cloth on the table, "are genuinely concerned about the solution to the problem of hunger in the free-enterprise system. They feel that it cannot be solved except through the system's producing the wealth that will be the source of dealing with the problem." He nods his head. "They are on good grounds there. After all, there's nothing to divide if there's no pie in the first place. Such men are, however, very concerned, and they do want to find the answers to this major problem."

Weakland's features, ordinarily calm and observant, light up as he leans forward. "They understood and reacted very well when I told them that the battle between capitalism and Communism was related not just to spheres of influence but to questions of values as well. Richard Nixon put it well in a speech a few years ago. He said that when the Russians go to countries in South America, they speak to the people of equality and brotherhood. When Americans go, they speak about Communism. After World War II, when America entered on this period of great international economic development, we always took our values with us—democratic notions and basic principles about human rights—the values we believed in and which we regarded as underpinning the economic system. As it turned out, we ended up supporting right-wing governments which did not respect these values. There has been a steady erosion of our export of these values, and now there is practically none left but that of profit."

Weakland pursues this theme, opening a fresh angle of vision on the pastoral letter's possibilities. "I tried to show these executives that our paper, with its Catholic bent, emphasizes values which appeal greatly to South America and Africa. In the long run, business will support what will be of help to it. That is why, ultimately, its representatives will endorse values. They are pragmatically good for business."

The archbishop snaps the thread of his concentration, nudged by a spirit friendlier than the ghosts of the old seminary, that of Benedictine hospitality. He smiles as he rises to send for some decaffeinated coffee, stretches, glances for a moment at the tundralike scene outside the windows. "One of the reasons capitalism has never taken deep root in South America is that its roots are too much in the Anglo-Saxon work ethic. It is in the interest of business leaders to rethink capitalism in terms of other ways of looking at the world. Just because American capitalism has failed recently to supply any value system to the world outside the United States is no reason that it cannot be done. Businessmen understand and respond well to this notion. It enables them to get out of their defensive mode."

Such business leaders do have criticisms, the archbishop notes, "on the section on poverty and employment. They criticized us bishops quite rightly for not including the notion of economic interdependence which we had mentioned earlier but which we seemed not to include there. They had never, however, thought of the Church as an international, interdependent body. These businessmen disagree on what we say about labor, denying that it is that way here." He gestures gracefully. "But it is in Korea, and the Church has to be aware of that. And we can't say anything that would harm Solidarity in Poland."

The archbishop serves decaffeinated coffee in mugs that bear the logo of the Milwaukee Catholic paper, smiling ironically at these further traces of diocesan commercial involvement. "Suddenly," he says, once more the teacher savoring his subject, "we are in a global world, and everything that happens everywhere is immediately known and lived through by all of us. Karl Rahner spoke of 'moments' in history, like that moment when the Church broke away from its Jewish origins, and another when it pulled away from its Greek roots. Rahner considered our time a new moment, the first era in which we are confronted with being a global Church. This was what Pope John XXIII emphasized, a world in which we could no longer think only in terms of our own self-interest. That is a theme that has been extended by Pope Paul VI and, repeatedly, by Pope John Paul II. It is this central realization that must inform all considerations, including economic ones, in this new age. No group, or country, or business can think only of itself anymore.

"Pope John Paul II has a deep consciousness of this, but he is caught in a bind because the Church in Central America has moved away from aristocratic domination. He has supported that but he cannot support any move toward Marxism. How to criticize certain aspects of liberation theology while still supporting the poor poses a very difficult problem for him."

Weakland leans back. "I'd like to say something about economics," he says, lowering his cup to the table. "The draft document is deficient in not having an economic conclusion. We must also include economists themselves in that section in which we describe those who are actors in the economy." He sips from his cup, weighs a judgment. "There are divisions among economists. Economics is undergoing a kind of a crisis, largely because of this factor of interdependence in the world. They have the data, but they lack the ability to predict from it. I see a threefold division here. First, there are economists who want to make economics a science, like physics. That is the economics that has been predominant in the United States. It has not proved helpful in the reality of American life.

"There is a second group of economists who, when it comes time for decision making, fall back on old-fashioned psychology. In particular, they return to Adam Smith, an eighteenth-century nonpsychologist. It's hard to imagine any other science turning back so far for a source to support its conclusions in the modern era." He shakes his head, smiles. "If there is one thing I have learned through this process, it is how much economics and psychology overlap. This economics is predicated on how people react emotionally. Often, however, people do not react in the way that they predict. The psychology behind this is very Anglo-Saxon, and, as I have said, that is why it is so difficult to transfer this imaginative structure of economics to South America."

Weakland is like a teacher anxious to share his latest intellectual understanding with his class. "Charles Murray's latest book, *Losing Ground,* is very statistical, but when he gets to the bottom line, as, for example, in regard to unemployed black youth, he interprets their mentality in Anglo-Saxon terms. He attributes their failure to get jobs to laziness. His thesis is that blacks and Hispanics have to come to think like us in order to enter the economy. That thought patterns other than his own exist never occurs to him. Michael Harrington has pointed out, for example, the black male's fear of failure as an alternate explanation for these same data. The Anglo-Saxon mind-set sees black women having babies out of wedlock as simply an activity for money. That these children are her possessions and sources of her dignity are notions they never even consider. Economics of this kind ends up being psychology, that of an Anglo-Saxon trying to solve a problem that is not necessarily Anglo-Saxon.

"The third group of economists sees the capitalist system as much freer and understands that a society's values can influence the way in which it functions. John Kenneth Galbraith, for example, is a representative of this kind of humanistic economist. You have to remember that John Stuart Mill said that capitalism can give you the laws of production, but not those of distribution. The laws of distribution have to come from other values."

The archbishop lifts his mug, holds it in midair. "The American capitalist system tries to be in the first category. It fails because it cannot be scientific in the way that physics is. It's no help if you try to transplant that system into other cultures that live by other value systems." He sips his coffee, speaks thoughtfully. "Japan is the great example of capitalism influenced by the nation's value system. Read their factory manuals, which speak of 'the dignity of the human person,' 'solidarity,' 'teamwork,' 'a sense of worth.' These are spoken of in a purely secular manner, but they are values that apply in their work."

Weakland, flooded with invitations to speak or preside at symposia inspired by the publication of the first draft of the pastoral letter, seems at peace in the eye of the hurricane of reaction that has blown almost without letup since the first draft of the pastoral was presented. "I think," he says dryly, "that the over-whelming reaction shows that we have hit a vital nerve, that this is a ripe area, and that we stepped in at the right moment." The mail, he says with good humor, has brought various kinds of criticism, some of it from individual people who are hurting badly because of the transformations now taking place in the American economy. "Other people," he says with a sigh, "have used this occasion to batter the Catholic Church, to bring out all their *ad hominem* arguments against Catholics. It makes me wonder how much anti-Catholicism still exists out there."

He sweeps a gesture. "Then there is an enormous amount of criticism from people who have not even read the draft. You get to know what they are think-ing, but that doesn't help the development of the document very much. Now more substantial criticism is coming in that is intellectually stimulating. They point out things with which I agree: We have to speak of the costs of programs of assistance to the govern-ment or to the private sector, we must address the problem of inflation, and the difficulties of job employment in an international, interdependent world." The archbishop smiles as if anxious to get on with the revision of the pastoral letter, the second draft of which is to be debated by the bishops at their meeting in Collegeville, Minnesota, in June 1985.

"We have a lot of different suggestions, but as to the form of the letter, we can't do everything that everybody wants us to do. We want to write a bishops' letter, a letter that the bishops will feel comfortable with, a *pastoral*, which is a literary genre all its own. We will necessarily put our greatest emphasis on human dignity, for that is where we truly are."

Weakland explains that a section on agriculture is now being added to the draft. "One of the problems," he says, returning to a difficulty he has noted in many of the criticisms made of the bishops' first version, "is that the standard method of thought in the United States is induction. You begin with the concrete. We, on the other hand, are deductive; we begin with principles, perhaps because that was our training in philosophy and theology. Americans are empirical, they want to address the problem as it exists rather than think out the implications of, for example, basic principles about the dignity of the human person. Many critics find it easy to agree with our principles, but that nod of agreement then allows them to disregard them. They tell you that the principles sound good but that they do not represent the real world, that empirical world they deal with pragmatically.

"Some critics suggest that we drop the applications," he says, bidding his visitor farewell. "If we did, however, we would miss the exercise in deductive reasoning that is so important. Theory has its own urgency, and if you commit yourself to thinking one through, you will change your life and the way you make decisions in the process."

FOUR

THE CRITICS OF THE AMERICAN BISHOPS

THE tough, steady, hardworking character of the American bishops has served them well throughout the conflict-ridden history of American Catholicism. They have often been in the middle of acrimonious disputes and have learned to absorb, if not to relish, criticism. They have needed their deep sense of confidence in their apostolic succession to withstand the vectors of force that press against them from all sides. They are currently the focus of the discontent of a mismatched bouquet of groups and interests, ranging from extremely conservative American Catholics, who think they have gone too far, to disgruntled liberals, who think that they will never go far enough. What are some of the charges that are currently leveled against the bishops?

These include criticisms from the two communities

affected by the bishops' recent pastoral letters, defense and business. Numerous examples of these have already been cited, especially the generalized notion that such fields are outside of the purview of the Catholic bishops. Some Catholics, including members of the self-appointed lay committee that issued its own dissenting letter on the economy just before the bishops' first draft was released, are convinced that the prelates err seriously whenever they step over the boundaries of the ecclesiastical world. They not only tend to embarrass themselves because of their inexperience, these critics aver, but they also violate the basic Catholic principle of subsidiarity, in accordance with which they should allow these matters to be dealt with at the lowest relevant levels of responsibility and authority. Such critiques are also expressed by such veteran liberal activists as Edward Marciniak of Loyola University in Chicago, who sees the bishops usurping the roles of concern that should be filled by Catholic lay people who are supposedly trained to express Catholic faith convictions in the public sector.

This tone inheres in some of the more friendly critical analyses of the first draft of the economic pastoral presented by such distinguished Catholic public figures as former Secretary of Health, Education, and Welfare Joseph Califano. In a typical "Yes, but . . ." comment, Califano writes: "The bishops are the moral and spiritual leaders of the largest block of Christians in the United States. Their attempt to write legislative programs and administrative regulations in their 'policy applications' subverts their powerful and desperately needed basic message . . . I hope the next draft . . . will stick to basics."

The conservative American press, particularly the *Wanderer* of St. Paul, Minnesota, attacks the bishops more vigorously and more basically. The *Wanderer*, for example, has led a campaign of unrelieved criticism of the present leaders of the American hierarchy, including Cardinal Bernardin and Archbishop Weakland. They have also assailed the USCC staff used by the bishops in preparing their letters, particularly the chief resource person, Father J. Bryan Hehir, whom they accuse of contaminating the research that has gone into the development of the pastorals on peace and the economy because of what they describe as his antecedent liberal bias. "He who frames the issue," says Dr. Edward Fuelner, a Catholic layman who directs the Washington-based Heritage Foundation, "goes a long way toward determining the outcome." Conservatives have also complained about the USCC staff's alleged liberal leanings in preparing the background material on which the bishops have based their criticisms of the Reagan administration's policy in Central America.

American bishops resent this criticism, especially when it is as broad as that of Edouard Cardinal Gagnon, pro-president of the Pontifical Council for the Family, who agreed with a *Wanderer* interviewer that, for a number of reasons, including its seeming independence, the American Catholic Church was in "material schism." U.S. bishops have expressed feelings of "being hurt" by such charges, which they brand as unfounded and insupportable. They also complain of the time they must spend explaining themselves to Roman congregations that have received letters of complaint inspired by such accusations. "We are bishops," one of them says, "and we are proud of what we have accomplished in these pastoral letters." Ironically, such papers as the *Wanderer,* which have encouraged letter-writing campaigns against the bishops, were just a generation ago the most vigorous defenders of the hierarchy and its authority.

Related to these doubts about their orthodoxy are the criticisms made by Roman officials concerning the bishops' collegial process of consultation in preparing their pastoral letters. The criticisms of Michel Schooyans cited in the first chapter are thought to reflect those of the Roman-based Bishop Jan Schotte, who, in the words of one bishop, was "the number one source of opposition to the U.S. bishops' 1983 peace letter." The latter was associated with the unexpected release to all American bishops of the supposedly confidential minutes of a January 1983 meeting in which a small U.S. delegation, including Bernardin, discussed the somewhat varying approaches of the American, French, and West German hierarchies to the application of general moral principles to specific issues, such as nuclear deterrence. The distribution was interpreted as an effort to influence the American discussions and the vote five months later on the final draft of the letter on war and peace.

The exhaustive, some say exhausting, process of preparing the pastoral letters has raised the eyebrows of some Roman curial officials, who fear that the conferences of bishops in different countries issuing documents that are in conflict, as the Americans were with the French and West Germans on the question of nuclear deterrence, may generate uncertainty about who speaks authentic doctrine. This was put into words by Joseph Cardinal Ratzinger in his 1984 interviews in the Milanese Catholic journal *Jesus*. He explicitly raised the issue of whether or not the national conferences of bishops were a threat to the central magisterial teaching authority of Rome. The cardinal, judged by many to be expressing papal reservations, also raised the issue employed by Rome in temporarily suspending the predecessor organization of the present conference of bishops over sixty years ago: the possible conflict between the autonomy of the bishop in his own diocese and the demands of an all-embracing national conference of bishops. He coupled these comments, which, according to leading American bishops, were aimed directly at the United States, with an attack on American theologians for allegedly accepting and incorporating instead of challenging contemporary cultural values in their work.

Pope John Paul II is thought to share the view of many European bishops that their American counterparts are too energetic—too American, in other words—to be taken seriously as intellectual leaders in the world Church. The Europeans are nettled by the American temperamental commitment to open discussion and debate—the habits of their lives in a pluralistic society—on questions of ecclesiastical policy. The West German bishops, for example, held no consultations before issuing their own letter on nuclear arms. Some Americans see a residual authoritarianism in such criticism of American democratic ways, a sentiment not greatly different from the one that inspired criticism of U.S. bishops for "Americanism" at the end of the last century. Some American Church leaders feel that many Roman officials still operate in regard to the United States with a long-outdated imaginative map. They cite, as an example, the original plan for the 1979 papal visit to America. Until revised to include a long arc into the Midwest, it was a pilgrimage to the major American cities of the Revolutionary era.

J. Brian Benestad, associate professor of theology at the University of Scranton, in Pennsylvania, has offered a consistently mannered criticism of recent efforts of the American bishops on grounds that they, or, more precisely their staff members, fail to appreciate the thrust of Pope John Paul's teachings on evangelization. The pope, Benestad says, emphasizes individual education in morals as a key to societal improvement rather than structural sociological changes brought about by political action. Benestad believes that the unanalyzed notion of "the moral issue" became a vague and imprecise motivation, a slogan used without deep reflection to justify the political activism of major religious groups during the 1960s. Salvation, in this view, flowed not from the conversion of individual hearts but from the politically effected transformation of national policies. In general, Benestad sees the bishops as somewhat unwitting hostages to a discredited liberal faith in the efficacy of policy statements based on the vague notions of a justifying and gratifying "moral imperative" about progress and reform.

Benestad argues that the National Catholic Welfare Council, the organization that preceded the present conference of bishops, put strong emphasis on character formation in and through all its vast educational and social programs. This individual spiritual development, he feels, is the essential step toward the organic society envisioned by medieval natural law thinkers. Virtuous individuals, like the leaven in the biblical yeast, change the institutions of society from within them. This distinctive Catholic outlook, while not disowned, has according to Benestad, been downplayed through the present national conference's apparent faith in and emphasis on what he terms "more generalized, culturally passing modes of intervention." This is rooted, as he sees it, both on the Catholic right and left, in a "secularist understanding of the Kingdom of God." Reflecting Cardinal Ratzinger's argument that American thinkers have been overly influenced by cultural fads, Benestad concludes that the "American hierarchy has not yet forged a close link between the pursuit of a peaceful and just social order and the affecting of individual hearts and minds through evangelization and education."

Benestad criticizes the bishops for pursuing justice through policy statements rather than evangelization, calling this strategy a failure to communicate the "true riches" of Catholic social teaching. The bishops, he claims, then adopt a "quasi-partisan" approach to politics by following an agenda of mainly liberal issues, such as economic and social equality, while ignoring issues in which conservatives express greater interest, such as the rise of materialism and individualism. The bishops, Benestad feels, also express great confidence in governmental intervention in their pastoral letters, statements, and testimony before Congress. Meanwhile, they fail to deal adequately, as he sees it, with the decline of religious belief and other contemporary spiritual problems. Suspecting that the bishops are "influenced by a desire to be relevant," he charges that, with the notable exception of their stand against abortion, the bishops tend to allow the secular world to set their political agenda. Even on the question of abortion Benestad criticizes the so-called "seamless garment" approach through which by Joseph Cardinal Bernardin seeks to link Catholic teaching on a wide number of pro-life issues, including abortion, nuclear war, and the death penalty. Benestad asserts that this program is based on a vague unifying ethic that fails to pay due heed to the formation of the virtuous individual as the foundation of true political and social reform.

Many American bishops consider Benestad's observations valuable but distorted in their assertions that they have scanted the question of the development of individual virtue that is so prominently emphasized by the pope. Not only do the prelates feel that their major pro-life effort goes against the grain of American culture, but they are convinced that it clearly shows their primary commitment to the dignity and value of the individual human person. Nor do the bishops feel that they are pawns of an excessively liberal support staff. That, as they see it, gives them little credit for understanding the principles and the programs supported by the bishops' conference. Leaders of the bishops also feel that the consultative process allows for a mix of opinions within the Catholic tradition and guarantees the representation of the sentiments of even those who most strongly dissent from their own positions. Of such give and take, as the Episcopal leaders see it, is effective collegial collaboration slowly fashioned. Only if the hierarchy lacked a process for dialogue could it be validly accused of constructing an agenda solely of "liberal" items.

Archbishop Rembert Weakland sees Benestad's criticisms as "vitiated" theologically by his failure to make a "differentiation of weight between documents voted on by the full assembly of bishops and statements of the officers of the conference, of staff members in their official capacity, or in lectures they may have given sometime or another. . . . A document voted on by the full conference of bishops certainly has more weight than a speech made by a staff member!" The archbishop also accuses the University of Scranton professor of choosing only one segment of the bishops' activity, "statements from one office; then he builds a theory around it." Weakland continues, "He faults the bishops for not being concerned about evangelization and justice education and for separating those concerns from the pursuit of justice. He makes no reference to any of the documents of the Bishops' Committee on the Liturgy, nor of the Bishops' Committee on Ecumenical Affairs even though they have profound effects on the Church as evangelizer." Weakland also mentions *The National Catechetical Directory for Catholics in the United States, Sharing the Light of Faith,* in which a "whole section is devoted to "Catechesis for Social Ministry." Stressing that the bishops' varied activities must be viewed as a whole, Weakland concludes that reading Benestad's book is "like going into the shoe section of a department store and then coming out upset because they did not sell shirts there."*

Benestad has continued his critical analysis of the bishops' activities in his examination of Joseph Cardinal Bernardin's call for a "seamless garment" of Cath-

---

*Rembert G. Weakland, O.S.B., *All God's People: Catholic Identity After the Second Vatican Council* (Mahwah, N.2.: Paulist Press, 1985, p. 197).

olic moral positions. "Many," he concludes, "consider a stress on virtue to be utopian, idealistic, ineffective. Consequently, the bishops would render a fine service to the country by clearly showing the connection between the practice of virtue and the quest for justice."†

The bishops are convinced that they have closely followed the teachings of the popes in the development of their recent pastorals. The draft document on the economy is strongly dependent on John Paul II's encyclical *Laborem Exercens,* and they remain confident of his basic support for their work. Still, many reported a certain noticeable diffidence in him during their *ad limina,* or regular five year visits to Rome in the summer of 1983. Eager to discuss their just-issued peace pastoral at the small group luncheons the pope held for them, they were surprised when he put them off by claiming that the had not yet had time to read that document fully. The papal hesitancy may, in the judgment of some, have been attributed to his sensitivity to European political conditions at the time, and of his desire not to allow a seeming endorsement of the American position to become involved in disputes about placing nuclear missiles on the continent.

American bishops have not been insensitive to the recent questions raised about the relationship of national conferences of bishops to individual dioceses.

†"Cardinal Bernardin and the Need for Catholic Social Teaching" in *Center Journal* (Notre Dame; Winter 1984, p. 27).

This familiar criticism, reiterated by Cardinal Ratzinger along with his skeptical comments about national conferences in general, illustrates, according to one bishop, Roman "mistrust for a superpower Church, which, like the superpower country it inhabits, commands a lot of attention because it is wealthy and powerful." Beneath these carefully phrased reservations one can detect, according to yet another bishop, "the curial struggle for control of Church teaching, which they see as threatened by national conferences who may seem too independent of Rome."

Jesuit theologian Avery Dulles has explored the theological foundations of national conferences of bishops, quoting an article Joseph Cardinal Ratzinger prepared as a theological expert at Vatican Council II in 1965. The latter had argued that it would be contrary to the collegial spirit for the individual bishop to isolate himself as a self-sufficient autocrat in governing a particular diocese. He maintained that it would be one-sided and unhistorical to maintain that "bishops' conferences lack all theological basis and could therefore not act in a way that would oblige the individual bishop." Dulles also cites Pope John Paul II's frequent observations on the close connection between bishops' conferences and the collegiality of the whole episcopate. Addressing the Brazilian bishops in 1980, for example, the pope said that "any utterance at all of a bishops' conference produces greater effect the more it is a reflection of unity as the soul of the episcopal collegiality as concretely incarnated in this group of bishops." Dulles notes that the Church has scores of other structures such as parishes, dioceses, and even curial congregations, that, although not mandated by divine law, nonetheless have been established by, and have authority from the Church. He concludes that "bishops' conferences have a solid theological basis in the principle of collegiality," but views the nature of their teaching authority as a separate question. Although in 1983 Cardinal Ratzinger denied that national conferences possessed any "mandate to teach," Dulles, after surveying tradition and history, sees their teaching authority as a practical reality. He holds that "the conference does have real doctrinal authority, but that authority varies enormously from one pronouncement to another. The bishops can and frequently do indicate what kind of obligation they intend to attach to their words."*

Archbishop Weakland defends the American bishops: "The allegation is that our consultative process suggests that we do not have all the answers and, therefore, that we weaken our authority and that of the magisterium by employing it. Those European critics want a strongly hierarchical model of the Church, in which the faithful are taught by the bishops, who have the gifts of the Spirit to give that authoritative teaching. The U.S. bishops believe in a

*"Bishops' Conference Documents: What Doctrinal Authority?" by Avery Dulles, S.J., *Origins,* Vol. 14 (January 24, 1985, pp. 531, 532).

model of the Church in which the Holy Spirit resides in all of its members and that the hierarchy must listen to what the Spirit is saying to the whole Church. That strengthens the teaching authority of the bishops as it ultimately does that of the magisterium. We emphasize discernment, not just innovation or self-reliance, as an integral part of the teaching process."

The American bishops have lived in an environment of intense criticism for several years. They have amply demonstrated their willingness to listen to and exchange views with sincere critics from every side. What their critics may underestimate is the bishops' sense of unity, their staying power, and their confidence that as bishops united with the pope they do not function without the guidance of the Spirit. Such elements guarantee a continuing dialogue, with an ever more careful refinement of theological and philosophical argument, on every issue the bishops may discuss in the future. Indeed, many feel that their process of consultation is ideally suited to promote a profound search of the Catholic tradition for what it can contribute to understanding contemporary ethical and moral dilemmas.

FIVE

JOHN CARDINAL O'CONNOR: THE PERSON IS THE CENTER

JOHN CARDINAL O'CONNOR stands in the middle of the dark paneled dining room of his residence just behind St. Patrick's Cathedral in New York City, a predecessor, John Hughes, a native of Philadelphia like O'Connor himself, watching attentively from an oil painting behind him. The sixty-five-year-old O'Connor, his straight-back brown hair only lightly threaded with gray, smiles patiently, a man who understands that crowds quiet down in sections rather than all at once. Around him, balancing their buffet supper plates as they pull away from their individual conversations, stand members of a committee of influential lay people who assist the archbishop of New York through raising funds and sharing their experience and counsel with him. The wealthy and powerful—bankers, lawyers, brokers, union leaders, and builders—are guests at a reception in honor of their varied contributions to the archdiocese, which, home to almost two million Catholics, transcends its own sprawling boundaries as a special presence in America's consciousness of Roman Catholicism.

Archbishop O'Connor who will be named a Cardinal a few months after this conversation, knits his forehead, touches a hand to the thin chain that drapes across his clerical vest. "I'm very grateful to all of you who, in so many ways, have contributed to the work of the Catholic Church here in New York. This diocese is, as you know, a microcosm of the Church in the whole country." The archbishop describes the suburban and farm areas that layer out beyond the intensely urbanized heart of Manhattan. "John Phelan here," O'Connor says, gesturing toward a dark-haired man a few feet away, "came to the Stock Exchange as a messenger boy forty years ago. He replaced a pneumatic tube. And now he is president of the New York Stock Exchange." As the good-natured laughter ebbs away, the archbishop cites other achievements of the members of the extraordinary gathering, tells them of his recent visit to Ethiopia, where, as he emphasizes, "I saw American aid getting through to the famine victims," thanks them for their help in this and many other matters.

O'Connor speaks urgently of the enormous problems of poverty that stretch from New York straight across the country. He found a bag lady on his own front steps a few evenings before. She refused his offers of food or indoor shelter, asking him only one question: "Is anybody else coming in this way tonight? Because I want to get some sleep." The archbishop pauses, glances upward as he must have at countless sets of church rafters in his forty years in the priesthood, twenty-seven of them as a Navy chaplain. "The bishops are now engaged in writing a pastoral letter on the American economy." His powerful listeners are practiced in not revealing their feelings in their facial expressions, but in the space of a pause, they lean forward slightly as the archbishop tugs the lanyard of the heavy artillery massed around him. "And I want to thank each and every one of you for the comments you have submitted to me about the first draft of that letter. I want to assure you that they have been sent along to the committee working on this letter, and that they will be reviewed very seriously and will be incorporated into the further development of this letter." His glance takes in the statuelike groupings. "I am confident that your expertise will be a great help to the bishops."

He concludes swiftly, moves among the men and women to thank them individually as they search out their hats and coats and begin to depart. It is near the end of another long day for O'Connor, who, since he became archbishop of New York in March 1984, has attained national prominence as a witty but forthright teacher of Catholic doctrine, viewed by many conservative Catholics as the man they had been waiting for ever since Vatican II shattered the majesty and constancy of their experience of the Catholic Church. A white-maned union leader in a camel-hair overcoat punches the air with a gesture as he recalls a long dead pastor from the Bronx. "He'd line 'em up," he hoarsely confides, "and there wouldn't be a peep out of them." Archbishop O'Connor gives him an understanding smile as he departs with the last of the guests.

Others have viewed the New York archbishop as the patriotic dissenter who, as a member of the committee of bishops that prepared its drafts, kept the pastoral letter on nuclear war from losing a sense of reality about the real world and its dangers. The archbishop has many times put his position in perspective for other interviewers, reiterating the fact that "I not only voted for it, I've tried to give it my forthright public support." He has emphasized the value of the process, involving public hearings and thorough discussion of all viewpoints, by which the drafts of that pastoral were written and revised, describing it as "indescribably helpful." As bishop of Scranton, Pennsylvania, where he served briefly before being appointed to New York, O'Connor led a massive educational campaign about the pastoral letter's meaning for the ordinary Catholic.

The archbishop confers briefly with one of his priest-aides, reviewing the ceremonies for the next morning's Ash Wednesday Mass, which he will offer, as he does every day, at 8 A.M. in the cathedral. He leads his guest to the second-floor corner room that served as an office for his immediate predecessor, Terence Cardinal Cooke. It is now a common room for the archbishop and his staff, and a large color photograph of him at a family Christmas celebration hangs on one wall. It is after 9 P.M. as he lowers himself onto a couch, removes his glasses, rubs his eyes, looks up as the housekeeper enters with trays of dinner. "So you've learned to cook at last, Maura," he says as he unfolds his napkin. He picks at the seafood and begins to speak about his efforts to stimulate discussion on the economy pastoral throughout the archdiocese.

"We have sent out a substantial number of copies of the first draft of the pastoral through the episcopal vicars and bishops. We have asked them to get them to the people. We synthesized the many responses we received and sent them on to the bishops' committee headquarters in Washington under four headings: city parishes, academic and religious, financial, and rural. We sent the raw responses that were sent in to us. I believe what we received reflects the great interest in this pastoral."

The archbishop sips a glass of white wine, speaks with great feeling. "Our credibility as bishops is very much at stake here. It is absolutely imperative—it's critical—that the second draft reflect the fact that we have looked at all these comments and suggestions and taken them seriously." He continues to eat lightly as he reflects on the impact of this letter-in-the-making. "Many wealthy people have read the first draft, and they really find nothing substantial to criticize in it. These are people who are familiar with the papal encyclicals and the Church's teaching on social issues. Even the critics support its thrust of concern for the poor. Others will say something like this: 'We completely agree with the objective, but from a technical point of view, if you carry out these recommendations in this way, you will wreck the economy.' There is no question, however, that even the first draft has raised people's consciousness about the problems of the poor."

He smiles, leans against the back of the couch, looks through the tall windows at the glittering Helmsley Palace Hotel that rises above the famous Villard House in which the archdiocesan offices were once located. "It's rare that you read in the critiques something like 'The bishops should mind their own business.' Those who do say this seem to think what we are doing is just political, or that we are seeking a new constituency among the poor, that kind of misinterpretation. That's not the kind of thing that I hear from Wall Street. They generally applaud the bishops for introducing a moral dimension into the discussions about the economy.

"I believe," he continues, leaning forward to pour some tea, "that as far as the National Conference of Catholic Bishops goes, this pastoral could go a long way toward furthering harmony among the bishops. That is, if, as I assume, the committee takes these incoming comments seriously and shows in its work that it has weighed them carefully. Then this pastoral will be a strong unifying force. I was one of the eight or ten bishops who got up on the floor of the conference in November to comment on the first draft. Every bishop —we varied a lot temperamentally—said something favorable about it. That interested me, that there was such a quick congealing of approval for it.

"So I think that it could further collegiality because more and more of us have become deeply concerned about the poor. In writing this pastoral, we are taking risks of being criticized as though we were just acting politically, or for our own interest. That risk always exists when you start critically addressing a system that by its very nature favors the wealthy. One risks alienating some people. The easy part is this: If you ask the rich to help the poor, they will say sure. But when you start addressing the structure and its built-in inequities, with, for example, so many persons living below the poverty level, that is something else. But the popes and the Vatican Council called for a correction of these inequities. The point is, the bishops have made a real commitment to the poor. We are now working out just how we are going to carry it out."

The archbishop's eyes are animated as he gestures. "Look at this house. I'd like not to have to live in it. I would like to live in a modest place, perhaps in the Bronx. But everybody says, 'You can't do that!' The archbishop of New York must be there, must meet his responsibilities to receive people, and so forth." His voice softens as he shakes his head. "Yet I go to sleep at night feeling very guilty that outside my door people are sleeping in the street." He sighs. "I don't know how to get at it. Many bishops feel the same way. It is a dilemma we haven't resolved."

He picks up his teacup. "So it may well be that because the bishops have made a real commitment to the poor—and if the pastoral letter is right and not just aphorisms—this work on the letter will be a unifying factor for the bishops."

A sweet, crinkling smile crosses his face as he hunches forward to speak thoughtfully. "I would make a distinction here. If we mean the bishops working together in harmony in their conference, I say this would enhance their collegiality. If we mean the United States Catholic Conference as a legal entity, a bureaucratic structure, that is something else.

"More and more thought is being given to the question of whether an ecclesial conference is a theological entity. There have been some papers, but in general the theological literature is thin in this area. Henri de Lubac," he says, referring to a famed French theologian, "has a chapter on national conferences in his book *The Church Our Mother*. He would say that national conferences have no ecclesiological authority or foundation. That also seems to be Cardinal Ratzinger's position. He strongly emphasizes the autonomy of the local bishop. Avery Dulles [an American Jesuit theologian] speaks of an 'evolving theology' of the conference of bishops. The theological status of national conferences of bishops is a knotty problem, but it is one that is in the air right now."

The archbishop loosens his clerical vest as he speaks

of the history of the NCCB and of the objections made to it during its early years as the NCWC after World War I. Rome, he suggests, feared the development of an "American Catholic Church in separatist form, something like a Gallican Church. The question of the conference's theological standing is a fascinating one. If I could choose to be part of a particular study group, I would select one that would examine this central question."

The archbishop nudges his tray onto the coffee table as I ask about Roman critics of the American bishops. "The Church in the United States is engaged in some very healthy discussions with the Holy See. 'Tension' is a strong word—perhaps we could describe it as a 'healthy tension.' You know, the Holy Father really *is* our father. He goes to bed thousands of miles away." O'Connor smiles. "Like any father, it's ten o'clock, do you know where your children are?

"Maybe," the archbishop continues, "the trick is to keep the rope taut. You don't want it slack, and you don't want to pull on it so hard that you snap it." He shifts on the couch. "I don't see any disputes between the Holy Father and the bishops, I don't see any there at all. But there are disputes between the bishops and various dicasteries in Rome. I think the accusation well founded that the Holy See would prefer dealing with one bishop rather than with the national conference. But that's not the issue. An ecclesial issue is developing. To what degree should a central authority in the United States be able to affect the autonomy of individual bishops? We could have an ironic paradox develop. Those who would resist encroachment from the Holy See could in turn attempt to impose a centralized bureaucratic structure on individual bishops in the United States."

Archbishop O'Connor flutes the fingers of his right hand as if pulling for the right phrase in the distinction he wishes to make between the NCCB and the USCC. "Are we talking about the staff? I don't say this critically. It is something in the nature of organizations. Staff people are working full time, and the bishops who are chairmen of the various committees are many miles away. They are not part of the day-to-day work or discussion. Such committees, then, by their very nature, inch by inch formulate the policies of the American Church. When the bishops convene, they address these policies—they reject, modify, or accept them—they have to make these judgments. Still, we have an obligation to intellectual integrity to make a distinction. Take, for example, a paper prepared by the staff on a specific subject. That's a pragmatic, working document, not a document to bind bishops. The individual bishops, after all, may be weighed down by their own work loads. Take a liturgical matter. We finally got the okay from Rome for communion under both bread and wine. I think that's great. The conference tells individual bishops they have permission. But the individual bishop must decide, as the pastor of his diocese, if it is for the good of the local church to use it. I'd like to see us do a preemptive study of the whole question before too many such studies accrue."

As the archbishop gestures, his ring, plain with a raised cross, glints in the subdued light. "If we examine our conference, we see that at the present time, the chief officers—the president, vice-president, and general secretary—see the Holy Father every year. That's great. It has helped very much in the conference. As that grows into a tradition, and as the Roman congregations get accustomed to dealing with the leadership of the conference, you might see the individual bishop feeling less and less immediately related to the Holy See and more related to the conference. Am I objecting to that? No, I'm raising a question. It seems likely that in five years that will grow. Will it be good for the Church? How does it affect the fundamental collegiality of the Holy Father with each individual bishop? Collegiality within the conference is secondary to that.

"I don't see this as a power grab," he continues, pouring tea for his guest, "but as a kind of organizational drift. Organizations tend to generate their own power. And as bishops are confronted with an increasing number of complex problems, they are glad to have an organization to support them. I'm chairman of the Committee on Social Development and World Peace. Two bishops have appealed to us to do a study on environmental waste. Neither feels he has the resources on his own, and it is a national problem. But

I can see that five years from now the NCCB might have a policy on environmental waste. Each bishop will feel compelled to go along. In this way a subtle shift could take place in the whole decision-making and policy-making process. I think it would be a serious mistake to approach this as if somebody were at fault. The question is, Is this the direction we want to go or not? Do we want a strong central government or a looser federation? That's of the nature of human affairs just as it was at the beginning of our own country." He grins, adds a thought. "As I understand it, the present structure drives partly from the management consulting firm of Booz Allen. It would be foolish to say that it is divinely inspired, or that it sprang from the forehead of a god. I'm saying we should anticipate the dynamics that take over precisely because the conference is a human organization." He leans forward as he asks rhetorically, "Is the national conference an ecclesial entity? I see that as perhaps *the* theological question of the next five years."

The archbishop settles back, studies the ceiling briefly before commenting on the criticisms that have been offered about the national conference by Professor J. Brian Benestad. "He feels that the social encyclicals and the pastoral letters are very important and well justified. But he also feels that we bishops have elided from forming moral principles, which is our forte, into what are dominantly sociological, structural recommendations. Benestad makes these criticisms in a very gentlemanly way because he believes that our contribution could be a quantum leap beyond what it is. I do not agree with all of Benestad's criticisms, but he is on to something. I believe that we have been a little apologetic in articulating our theological views.

"Another thing that he emphasizes is the relationship between persons and structures. It is clear that he is well grounded in the writings of Pope John Paul II. I have a hypothesis that you cannot understand Pope John Paul's encyclicals without understanding his concept of humanistic phenomenology. In *Redemptor Hominis,* for example, man is the way for the Church and for all of society." O'Connor speaks enthusiastically now as he closes on a theme that is central in his own outlook. "The pope is terribly sensitive to the danger of subordinating the person to any structures, no matter what they are. As a result, he has a form of liberation theology that is mind-boggling. It won my sympathy immediately. In an early paragraph of the draft letter on the economy we find the crucial question: What does this do to and for the human person? Everything else could be erroneous, and yet that's the thing. That is what I teach myself, what I keep repeating. That is what I told Wall Street. What does the economy do for and to the human person?"

The archbishop crosses one leg over the other, grasps his foot as he continues, his weariness overcome by his interest in the question he is pursuing. "How can we get at this? There's a place for macroeconomics, but when you're trying to change a piece of society, you have to think in other terms, as the economic philosopher E. F. Schumacher did when he spoke of 'small is beautiful.' When the chips are down, any given chip of society contains all its elements, ethnicity, and everything else. As I see it, that's the parish level. You have to respect the way the pastor runs his parish when he knows his people and their needs and customs. In the same way, the role of the individual bishops must be respected even by the Holy See. They may say, 'Here is the Code of Canon Law. Operate within this framework.' What these notions come back to is that we are always dealing with the human person, that we must always minister to that person as a person."

Archbishop O'Connor tests his now cold tea, and warms it up. "My suspicion about the pastoral on the economy is that the one thing the committee members will be asked to look at most seriously is the idea of the dependence they seem to be generating on the government.

"I think we need a healthy distrust of government, any government. To build too much of your economy on social welfare or government is a mistake. The government has a role, but, historically, do governments take care of their people? No. We have to be careful about predicating too much on government. Take the health care in the archdiocese. It costs a billion dollars a year. Three quarters of that comes from third-party payments from the federal, state, or city governments. Talk to doctors. They spend too much of their time on governmental regulations."

The archbishop leans forward, deep concern underlining his words. "The new administration in Washington says that it can't afford health-care subsidies. But a health-care empire has been built on third-party payments. What happens? People close down or sell out to private entrepreneurs, who treat health care strictly as a business." He shakes his head slowly. "In the areas of health care and education, if the government is hostile, you do not know what conditions they will impose for receiving support. I have a perfect example here in New York in Executive Order 50." He refers to his well-publicized unwillingness to comply with an order of New York Mayor Ed Koch that there be no discrimination against hiring homosexuals by archdiocesan agencies that do business with the city. "I have nothing *per se* against homosexuals," he says earnestly, "and one half of our budget of one hundred and thirty two million dollars for services comes from the city. They say that unless we follow their policy, we will lose city and county funding. Our position is that unless we can run our agencies without government control, we don't want your money.

"It's a question of control. I have told the mayor that we are prepared to hire those of homosexual orientation, whether it is in the present, the past, or in the future. But we want to make our decisions on a case by case basis. Think of it in relationship to another ACLU [American Civil Liberties Union] suit against the city for giving contracts to religious agencies. They demand that we meet pages and pages of regulations. The city has come to an agreement with the ACLU that requires the availability of abortion counseling and the removal from agencies of all excessive signs of religion. How might that be interpreted? What might be forced on us in the future?" (A few months later O'Connor's position will be vindicated by the courts. Shortly after that he will make his pastoral concern for the person clear by calling for the establishment of a center in which the victims of AIDS, many of them homosexual, and often rejected and turned out by hospitals and other institutions, will find a place of guaranteed treatment. Mother Teresa will oversee the project, which will be staffed by members of her religious order. Homosexual activists will welcome his plan but seem to remain uncertain about O'Connor, even though he is one of the few public figures to implement pastoral care in this concrete way. Though progress on this front has been temporarily delayed, the new cardinal remains publicly optimistic about the future of such a hospice.)

O'Connor shifts his position slightly as he continues, "My concern is that we are no longer able to act directly out of charity in responding to the needs of the people. That's why I have been holding meetings on alternative health care, so that we might restore that sense of charity. Mother Teresa wouldn't be permitted in New York City to do her direct, loving work for the destitute and the incurable. And if I took someone off the streets and put them to bed here and he died during the night, I'm told that I would be subject to lawsuits." He knits his brow, gazes intensely, as a surgeon might who has at last uncovered the site of a massive infection. "And if I let women leave their children during the day at the diocesan offices, the board of health and the unions—and I'm a big union man—would move right in on me. The unions here turned down Mother Teresa's offer to help."

The archbishop rises, walks to the window. "What I wonder is whether *ab initio* it would be possible to rediscover charity, that is, to restore direct service to others out of love, maybe even on a shoestring." He turns back, smiles, looks at his watch. It has grown late and he still wants to read a sheaf of parish reports. Archbishop O'Connor waves goodnight and climbs the stairs, a man slightly stooped under the weight of his major concerns. He has lived in and supported major institutions throughout his life: the Catholic Church, the United States Navy, the Military Ordinariate, the NCCB, and the archdiocese of New York. But his first commitment is clearly to the persons who may be easily lost in the bureaucratic mazes that grow naturally from such institutions. The person, not the structure, remains the central focus of his life and work.

SIX

JOSEPH CARDINAL BERNARDIN: A COMMITMENT TO THE COLLEGIAL CHURCH

The traditional residence of Chicago's archbishop stands on the Near North side of the city facing Lincoln Park. Darkened and mysterious for many years when John Cardinal Cody lived there alone, it is now brightly lit and busy as the home for Joseph Cardinal Bernardin and several priests who work with him in the administration of one of the largest and most important archdioceses in the Catholic Church. The fifty-seven-year-old cardinal, who served as general secretary of the NCCB during the years of its restructuring under John Cardinal Dearden, came to Chicago in 1982 after almost ten years as the archbishop of Cincinnati. He has also served as president of the NCCB and, much in the pattern of Dearden, whom he counts along with the late Archbishop Paul Hallinan of Atlanta as his mentors, is regarded by the great majority of his fellow bishops as a highly credible figure, a leader whom they trust. He chaired the committee that drafted the 1983 pastoral letter "The Challenge of Peace," a document that gained international attention. Brother bishops regard his commitment to the implementation of the process of collegial discussion and consultation as crucial to the successful drafting of that letter.

Cardinal Bernardin eases himself into his desk chair in the small office off his rooms. He broke his right collarbone in a fall on the winter ice and wears his obviously still tender arm in a sling. The wall behind him is covered with framed pictures, some modern and some traditional, some religious and some secular, a collection that reflects the taste and style of a man who sees the Church not set against the world but in its very midst. "There are two reasons," he says thoughtfully, "that the recent pastoral letters have attracted so much media attention, much more, for example, than the bishops' 1979 letter on racism. The first is that these newer letters have been prepared through an extensive process that involves many people and ensures that the bishops are deeply involved in its development. Second, the topics seem to have a greater degree of immediacy in the mind of the general public. The people wanted to talk and hear about the subject of nuclear war—it was very much their concern at the time we were working on the

letter. I don't mean in any way to play down the evil
or urgency of racism—and I don't think we have
done enough to get more attention paid to that pastoral—but I believe that these are the *de facto* reasons.
Nuclear war was a topic whose time had come, and
it transcended denominational lines. The bishops'
open process of working on it gave it a great deal of
visibility. So too with the pastoral being developed on
the economy. That is a topic on the front burner
because the economy affects everybody."

He adjusts himself in the chair, gazes through the
tall window toward the park beyond. "One of the
criticisms some people make is that in the development of these letters the bishops are really under the
influence of the staff of the United States Catholic
Conference. This comes up frequently. These critics
give the impression that we bishops cannot think for
ourselves." He turns toward his visitor, his voice firm
with conviction. "This picture of the bishops being at
the mercy of a staff of liberal bent is simply not true."
His tone becomes gentle, reflective again. "I don't
know if these critics really believe this, or whether it
is just a way they have of attacking the bishops. In
preparing our major documents we go through such
an extensive process that it is simply wrong to give
the impression that the bishops are not fully responsible for the final document."

The cardinal adjusts his sling as he continues, "Take
the war and peace pastoral. We had the same complaints about staff domination in that as Archbishop

Weakland's committee is getting in its work on the economic letter. It is true that we worked with staff members and many consultants, but the five bishops on that commission worked very, very hard. The whole committee of bishops and their consultants went tirelessly through hundreds of pages of commentary after the first two drafts were presented. Most of the redrafting was done in the context of these suggestions. Then, when we met as the official conference of bishops in May 1983, there were over five hundred amendments that we considered on the floor as a group. The final document was passed by a 238 to 9 vote. To maintain that we were manipulated and that the document represented the thinking of those other than the bishops is simply incorrect."

Cardinal Bernardin pauses to take a phone call about the trip he must make in a few days to Rome in his capacity as a member of the council of the secretariat of the synod to work on the agenda for the synod of world bishops that is to meet there in the fall. On another wall hang framed documents of his appointment as a bishop, and in the corner space by the window, photographs of his investiture as a cardinal by Pope John Paul II in January 1983. The room, decorated in muted colors, speaks in tones as soft and measured as his own of a man comfortable with his position and responsibilities. The cardinal hangs up the phone, picks up his theme. "The first draft of the economics pastoral received a great deal of criticism. That draft was, of course, the work of a small group of bishops, staff members, and consultants. By now, however, all the bishops have reacted. I personally sent ten pages of comments. The second draft will be different because of all this input, and the third draft will, because of additional revisions based on advice from all the bishops and others, be different from the second. Ultimately we will come up with what the bishops want to say. And we are determined to do this publicly and to let the world know how we voted.

"This process is aimed at getting the maximum participation in the development of these pastoral letters. This process requires the bishops to immerse themselves in the relevant materials. There is no other way that one can participate except by becoming thoroughly familiar with the issues that are involved. If I didn't, for example, go through this process on the economic letter, and only received the draft of the letter just before the meeting, then one could argue that the document is not the work of the bishops. But this is simply not so."

The cardinal shifts in his chair, gesturing with his left hand. "It was amazing to see how much work the bishops had put into the peace pastoral, and how actively involved in the process they were. The same process is being followed with the economic letter. There has been extensive consultation with experts of all kinds and numerous public hearings. Now I realize that those who would come to such public hearings are those who are frequently socially active among the poor, so about seventy percent of those at such hear-

ings support the document as it is in the process of
development. Persons with different economic
philosophies normally do not come to such hearings.
But we have plenty of input from CEOs and other
business leaders. I, for example, in preparing my own
comments on the first draft of the pastoral, had a
private meeting with a number of Chicago's leading
business executives and professional people. I also attended, along with Archbishop Weakland, a meeting
at Morristown, New Jersey, earlier this year with the
heads of eighteen of the largest corporations in America. We had a very good discussion with them about
the pastoral. On the basis of all that, and my own
experience and reading, I have sent in my comments
to the committee. The process will work the same
way with the second draft."

Bernardin pauses, a teacher underscoring a point.
"The very nature of this collegial process, in which
the other bishops are as deeply involved as I myself
am, guarantees that the pastoral letter will come from
the bishops themselves, that it cannot be the work of
just a few people. Only if we had a truncated process
could one argue that the bishops were not sufficiently
involved, or that the letter was composed essentially
by members of the USCC staff. I am convinced that
this process is as important as the product that comes
from it. It has enormous educative value for the whole
community.

"When Archbishop John Roach [St. Paul], then
the president of the bishops' conference, and I at-

tended a meeting in Rome in January 1983 about the peace pastoral, one of the questions we were asked was, Why do you Americans use such a process? Wouldn't it be better to get a consensus among the bishops privately and then present this to the public? We explained that we were using our process deliberately, that the question of war and peace belonged to the social order, that it was not merely an ecclesial problem, and, therefore, not to consult a broad cross section would take away from its credibility. Second, it was our position that the process in itself had value. It sensitizes people to the problem, and one cannot be a part of the process without learning about the subject and seriously reflecting on its moral implications."

The cardinal emphasizes that following a proven process not only improves the outcome but takes the focus off individual personalities so that they, for reasons that have little relationship with the issues, do not determine the results of a given discussion. Bernardin is quite aware of the criticism that has been directed toward one of the priest staff members of the USCC, Father J. Bryan Hehir, who has worked intimately on the development of both the peace and the economic pastorals. "Such criticisms," the cardinal says, letting his chair turn half an arc, "are in the very nature of bureaucratic life, but Bryan Hehir is one of the most intelligent, loyal, and committed persons I have ever known or worked with. It is because of his competence and his marvelous analytical mind that he is of such great value. Beyond that, he is a very good priest, who exercises his priestly ministry in an extraordinary way. He is very active at the pastoral level. Furthermore, Father Hehir is extremely loyal to the Church; he places himself at the service of the bishops, and he has never done or said anything to undermine them. He is a very candid person, who will tell you, 'Here are the implications of this position, but it is your decision to make.' There is really *no* substantiated criticism of Father Hehir."

The cardinal is also aware of the criticism of his own positions, especially of his support, as chairman of the pro-life committee of the bishops, for what he describes as the "linkage" between all the issues that bear directly on the dignity and value of human life. In what has become a famous speech given at New York's Fordham University in December 1983, the cardinal, drawing on the implications of the recently passed pastoral letter on peace, explored the connection between the Catholic teaching on war and the Catholic teaching on abortion. "Both," he said, "must be seen in the light of an attitude of respect for life. The more explicit connection is based on the principle which prohibits the directly intended taking of innocent human life." This he used as the foundation for beginning an inquiry into the relationship between the "right to life" issues and the "quality of life" issues, suggesting that "the Catholic position on abortion demands of us and of society that we seek to influence a heroic social ethic." Arguing that consistency demanded a commitment to a range of pro-life issues that included protecting the unborn, reducing the arms race, standing against euthanasia, and ending capital punishment, Bernardin said that such issues, different yet profoundly related, constituted a "seamless garment" that called for a new consensus in the Church as well as in society at large in terms of shaping public policy according to the traditional Catholic moral vision.

He has since been accused of weakening pro-life activities, of being "soft" on abortion, because of his effort to identify the linkage among the questions relating to the sanctity of life. The cardinal has been accused of putting anti-abortion activities on the same plane with seeking nutritional programs for schoolchildren and has been the subject of letter-writing campaigns and regular attacks in the right-wing Catholic press. "People who do not accept the consistent ethic of life theme," he says slowly, "do not seem to understand it. They think I am saying something that I am not saying. Others know what I am saying and disagree with my position.

"The consistent ethic of life theme is based on a fundamental moral value, namely the sacredness of human life and our responsibility to protect and promote human life. Take that value away and there is nothing left. The ethic shows a linkage among these issues, but it does not collapse all these issues into one, nor does it propose one solution for all these problems. While there is linkage, each of these issues is different, and each requires its own distinct moral analysis, and each requires its own moral solution. As teachers, we bishops try to provide a moral vision that highlights the relationship among these issues and also highlights the fact that if you do not support one of them, you might be undermining another of them.

"I do not equate capital punishment with abortion. A consistent ethic of life does not put the problem of taking life in abortion and war on the same plane with the problem of promoting individual dignity through, for example, humane programs of nutrition, health care, and housing. But a consistent ethic identifies both the protection of life and its promotion as moral questions. It argues for a continuum of life which must be sustained in the face of diverse and distinct threats from different sources. This consistent ethic does say that as individuals and groups pursue one issue, whether it is in opposing abortion or capital punishment, the way they oppose one threat should be related to support for a systemic vision of life. Consistency does rule out contradictory moral positions about the unique value of human life. No one is called to do *everything,* but each of us can do *something.* And I think we can try not to stand against each other when the protection and the promotion of life are at stake."

The cardinal's convictions are not unrelated to those of his brother bishops. When he gave his report on the work of his pro-life committee at the bishops' meeting in November 1984, Bernardin was clear about the position that he felt best reflected that of the

NCCB. He concluded his report by saying, "I maintain that, both conceptually and as a matter of political strategy, the consistent ethic strengthens our overall pro-life position and motivates us to pursue each issue vigorously. It gives us credibility and greater moral authority when we hold up, for the entire world to see, a moral vision which does not permit our respect for life to be eroded at any juncture . . . I am convinced that this is the direction in which you wish our committee to proceed . . . This is a *new moment* for us. We will not flinch from our sacred duty to protect the unborn, nor will we be deterred in speaking out in defense of life wherever it is threatened or violated." The assembled bishops, in the closest thing to a collegial endorsement possible in the circumstances, rose and gave Cardinal Bernardin a standing ovation.

Bernardin moves his right arm as carefully as the bishops must proceed in their program of calling upon the Catholic community in America to think deeply about the relationship between faith and the major cultural problems of the day. "Some people tell the bishops," he says in the tones of a man who has heard this advice often, "*stay in the sanctuary* and preach the Gospel. But we are not slighting the sacramental aspects of Catholic life, and we are not abandoning our tradition of building virtue in people. We are saying that there is more responsibility for Catholics than some people want to admit. A mature religious outlook requires persons to inspect their lives in their entirely. In our pastoral letters we bishops are inviting people into a public meditation on what an integrated religious life really is.

"Some critics say that we bishops no longer emphasize the development of individual character. That is simply not so. We still have an obligation for the formation of individual consciences, so that persons can carry out their functions and responsibilities in life. But a significant thing has happened in Catholic history. Vatican II, especially in the document *The Church in the Modern World*, teaches that in addition to the formation of individual consciences, we must face the major issues that confront our society. The role of secular society is different from ours, but we exist within that society, and we must address its social structures, always from a moral perspective."

Bernardin nods toward a portrait of the present pope. "In the document *Gaudium et Spes*, in which the role of the Church in the modern world is discussed, in the encyclicals of the recent popes—John XXIII, Paul VI, and John Paul II—we find that they do not focus only on the formation of individual consciences. The present Holy Father brings these two aspects of life—individual conscience and social responsibility —together all the time. The idea that these two spheres are separate is incorrect. As far as the pope and the bishops go, they have integrated the teachings of Vatican II, but we find some critics who resist doing this." The cardinal pauses, leans forward slightly, speaks like a man coming to an important point.

"*That's* what all the fuss is about: Some critics don't want us to talk about social problems, they only want us to speak about individual morality."

The cardinal takes another phone call, then turns to another critical theme that is often sounded against the American bishops. "Some people say that we have substituted policy statements for evangelization. I insist that the perspective we must take is moral, not political, when we urge certain policies. We do not operate in a vacuum, and at times our position will be the same as that of one or the other political party. We are against abortion, so at times we are identified with the political faction that is also against it. We are against something else and we will be said to identify with the party that espouses that position, whatever it is. But it's our responsibility to address *all* these issues, whatever they may be, from a moral perspective, and you simply cannot equate that with a purely political statement. The overlap is inevitable, but that cannot keep the bishops from speaking out on the moral dimension of the issues of our day."

There is a hint of timelessness in the utterly silent old house that was erected in the days of Catholic authoritarian glory. Bernardin smiles as his visitor raises the question of Roman criticisms of the American bishops and their collegial process as though he and the walls had heard these charges often. "Episcopal conferences," he says evenly, "are a product of the Second Vatican Council. Sometimes people give the impression that they came out of nowhere. Vatican II called for this national or regional collaboration. National conferences come from the Church itself. One of the reasons for this collaboration is that we live in a highly interdependent world; it is also true that we are interdependent at regional levels as well. It is important, therefore, that there be the exchange and working together that an episcopal conference provides. I have welcomed the development of these conferences, and I speak from having had the experience of serving as president as well as general secretary of the American conference. No one has envisioned that an episcopal conference such as ours would become a superchurch and displace the local church, or in some way usurp the individual bishop's personal relationship to the pope. That was never intended.

"I think that the task is to maintain a certain balance. If in fact the episcopal conference tended to become a superchurch so that the local bishop lost his autonomy, I would be the first one to criticize it. That is not the nature of the National Conference of Catholic Bishops and is not the way that it functions. One must work to keep one's balance in everything in life. Some of the critics of the conference have never had my experience inside the conference, and my own feeling is that I am not at all hampered as an individual bishop by a conference that, in fact, is a great asset."

The cardinal rises slowly to escort his visitor out, still reflecting on the nature of the conference of bishops. "I do not deny the potential for problems, but I do not think that we have them with our conference, that the critics, wherever they are, are raising a false issue." His phone is ringing again back in his office. Standing at the top of the staircase, his bound arm giving him the look of a commander who is no stranger to the trenches, Bernardin pauses and speaks reflectively. "Each bishop has a responsibility to teach the Gospel. To the extent that we speak together, we enhance our moral authority as teachers. *That* is what being a bishop is all about."

SEVEN

FATHER THEODORE M. HESBURGH: THE VIEW FROM NOTRE DAME

FATHER THEODORE HESBURGH has served as president of Notre Dame, perhaps the most famous Catholic university in the world, since 1952. He is, in the judgment of many, the best known and most influential Catholic priest in America. He has worked as an educator and administrator and has served as chairman of the Carnegie Foundation, as delegate to the Atoms for Peace conferences in Vienna, on the Civil Rights Commission, and in scores of other national and international posts. At sixty-seven, he remains vigorous and trim, his strong familiar features set off by the silver edges of his wavy black hair. He settles against the back of a booth in the Morris Inn at the edge of the university campus, smiles up at the waitress, orders an omelet. Spread across the wall behind him is a mural depicting the campus in 1844.

"There has been a sea change in the bishops of the United States," he says in easy, confident tones. "A generation ago the bishop of a diocese was usually seen as a remote hierarch wearing a gold miter and a lace surplice and holding a crosier in his hand, and he was seen on rare, formal occasions and mostly at a distance. Bishops of a previous age lived in big houses they called palaces, after the old Roman style, and they tended to dominate the idea of the Church, indeed, to *be* the Church. The Catholic papers would be filled with their pictures, and it seemed that whatever was done in the Church was done by them." He shakes his head, smiles at his own recollection. "That was the era of great personalities in the hierarchy, men like Mundelein of Chicago, who was famous as a friend of Franklin D. Roosevelt, and O'Connell of Boston and Dougherty of Philadelphia, regal patriarchal figures who ruled as complete autocrats. Add Cardinal Spellman to that list, and possibly Cardinal Cushing, and you have the men who practically dominated the American Church up until the time of Vatican II." He crumbles a Saltine into his soup. "That says something about the nature of the Church in that era.

"Then something happened that changed the whole character of the American Church. From a Church almost solely identified with the hierarchy, it became understood theologically as a People of God, and the bishops transformed themselves from authoritarian patriarchs into servants of the servants of God. They are seen now as part of the Church, but not the whole of it." He interrupts himself, speaking enthusiastically. "Take a picture I saw in the *National Catholic Reporter* just this week. It is worth a thousand words in describing the changes that have taken place in the bishops and in the development of their national conference. The picture shows a group of men praying at the tomb of Archbishop Romero in El Salvador. They are informally dressed and yet they are the most important archbishops in the United States—Cardinal Bernardin of Chicago and Archbishop O'Connor of New York—and they are in their shirtsleeves praying for a martyred brother bishop. It's impossible to imagine such a picture being taken a generation ago. It shows a changed life-style, a changed sense of their role as they demonstrate international concern for a country that old-fashioned bishops would never have even thought of visiting. They show that they are moved by Archbishop Romero's struggle for justice and peace, and they show that they are trying to get some sense of what is just and what isn't in this Central American country."

Fully animated, Hesburgh holds his spoon just above his cup of soup. "Think of the letter sent by the president of the bishops, Jim Malone of Youngstown, Ohio, to all the members of Congress asking them to vote against the MX missile. A pretty good letter! I think the bishops had to send it because in their pastoral on nuclear war they expressed a very strictly conditioned acceptance of nuclear weapons as deterrents.

Here in the MX we have an offensive, first-strike weapon with enormous power and accuracy, and it is so big it is almost impossible to hide. It is, therefore, vulnerable and practically invites attack. If the bishops had kept quiet in the face of that, they would have lost their credibility as religious leaders. But the point is that they have been consistent, they have followed through on their pastoral letter, they have spoken out on an issue with enormous moral implications."

He lowers the soup untasted to his plate. "I think that's why bishop baiting, which used to be a favorite indoor sport of the clergy, has almost disappeared. It's because we have this new kind of bishop who responds strongly to Vatican II's vision of the Church. Take our own experience here at Notre Dame. For the first one hundred and fifty years of the university's existence the only time we had a bishop here was on some big occasion, and he would be dressed up and remote to the students. The bishop who has just retired, Bill McManus, would often come in a pastoral role to the campus, say Mass in one of the halls, and hear confessions in the church. He was in that confessional one night from seven P.M. until one A.M. The students now see bishops as pastors who are not at a distance at all. That educates them to what the new Church really is." The university president waves a greeting across the dining hall, samples his food, describing between bites the active presence of Bishop McManus on many levels of Notre Dame life. "Nobody around here has to ask *what is a bishop* because they've known him as a religious leader, a man who preached and practiced social justice, a man always trying to learn."

Father Hesburgh leans back as he goes on, "Post–Vatican II bishops must be pastors fundamentally. Instead of being remote figures pronouncing the last word on everything, they must be accessible and be in the thick of things. On top of that, today's bishops must be skilled executives, and they are never easy to find, because they are running corporations. He has religious professionals, his priests, whom he must manage." Hesburgh smiles ruefully. "And they are difficult to handle. If you survey the new Church, you'll see that sixty to seventy percent of what old-fashioned pastors did is now being done by lay persons. They constitute a new layer with whom the bishop must deal, and they give him plenty of input and advice. The contemporary bishop must also be a good spokesman for the Church. The old days of 'no comment' are long gone. Reporters will drive religious leaders to the wall these days, so that makes for a very changed world as well."

Father Hesburgh pauses as the waitress delivers his omelet. He asks her about her family, then returns to the subject of the demands made on modern bishops. "Put that all together and I think it's remarkable that the bishop's job can be handled at all. It works best, of course, when the bishop facilitates the work of others and does not, like so many bishops of other days, stand at center stage all the time. Bishops function very well as they pick up good people to handle subsidiary tasks. That's one thing that should be said about Cardinal Spellman, by the way. He knew how to give responsibility to other people, and he didn't let small things or petty feelings stand in his way. Bishops who can't follow that path will certainly fail in this age. They simply cannot be the whole show anymore, and they must surround themselves with able co-workers. This is really an application of collegiality on the local level. The principle must be applied at every level, international, national, and on the local scene."

Hesburgh gestures with his fork, as he must have done with chalk when as a young priest he taught theology at Notre Dame. "The basic authority of the bishop is, therefore, seldom exercised as it was in the past because it is spread over so many people. The bishops preserve and enhance their authority by not using it unilaterally. There is a real sharing of responsibility with many other persons, and bishops support and praise them, and let them take the credit when it is their due. This collegial style does fit the modern Church very well.

"The American bishops are really saying something to the rest of the world by showing how the concept of the Church as the People of God can be made operative. It's especially important that they are giving new places to women in the work and ministry of the Church. Just look at today's Church and see how many activities once reserved to priests are now being done by lay people. Rome uses lay people in these ways very little. The American nuns are prime examples of women ready and able to take on increased responsibility in today's Church. The heart of it is the way in which the bishops use their authority; that is, they use it well by hardly using it at all.

"Power is always best used when it is used least. These modern bishops are very careful about that, and they are also leery of the trappings of power that previous generations seemed to love. The bishops, by their restraint in using authority, have solved a problem that American industry hasn't as yet: how to make power sharing work through practical collegiality." The university president chats briefly with a friend who has crossed the restaurant to say hello, then turns to a personal example of his experience of a changed Church. He describes his brother and sister-in-law, who are both Eucharistic ministers in their parish. His brother also heads the finance committee, and his sister-in-law conducts an active ministry of visitation and brings the Eucharist to nearby nursing homes. That so much practical authority and sacramental ministry is now in the hands of lay persons illustrates the broad and positive changes that have taken place throughout the country. "When I say Mass there," he says with a grin, "and they help distribute the Eucharist, people think it's a family affair."

Hesburgh nudges his plate aside. "What people should appreciate is that the Catholic Church in the United States is not falling apart but restructuring itself as a much better church. It really is functioning as a People of God." He pauses for a moment. "I think our experience here at Notre Dame is predictive of how things will develop, for example, in vocations to the priesthood. We are getting candidates at an older age, many with advanced degrees. I think they choose the priesthood because they see what the new Church is like in their years here. Not only is the Church spared the need to give these candidates a basic education, but their survival rate is much greater. When we had huge crowds entering, we also had large numbers leaving. Now that will change dramatically. What I think they see here—and in the new Church in general—is the availability of priests and religious [brothers], that the Church is a community that cares and is open to them and their concerns. I think that is the paradigm for the parish of the future. It will be a place where people can find care for their spiritual needs. It won't be like the old-fashioned parish with its forbidding and highly clerical rectory. People used to be scared just by the look of the place. Today's bishops are very different from that glacial hierarchical overlay that demanded of the laity: Pray, pay, and obey."

He smiles at the ironic memory tracings of a long-vanished era in American Catholic life, pours coffee for his guest, who asks him about his predictions for the future. "That is a picture of the Church that simply did not exist when I was a kid. The present openness was unthinkable at that time. I would base my predictions around these roots. The basic feature is that the bishops have opened the Church up and that more and more people will become actively involved in its work, from thinking out moral positions on urgent issues to helping in sacramental ministry. These changes are already in place. They have been since the Council, and while, as at any other time of great change, there are excesses and failures, the truth is that the Church is much stronger than it has been in a long time. This generation of bishops fits right into this new open Church. These men have the spirit of the Council, they see themselves not as overlords but as servants. They understand that the only important power is out there in the people, and they have been trying to harness that as builders of dams do with great rivers, transforming it into useful energy. There is no doubt that there is a certain messiness around the edges, but that's to be expected. We have left the age of believing and confessing by rote; we are inviting people into a much more mature understanding of faith and responsible practice of it in their lives."

Father Hesburgh leans forward, his coffee forgotten. "I believe with Rahner that we are at a critical point in Church history. It is now an international Catholic Church, and it has to come to grips with that reality. Take China, for example, in which one out of every four human beings lives. We can't act as if they do not exist. The Church needs a whole new *modus agendi* in dealing with this great people. It must accommodate itself to that culture. It must accommodate and support the Catholicism that is already there." Hesburgh refers to the Chinese Patriotic Church, whose leaders were excommunicated many years ago for wanting a say in nominating their own bishops. His face clouds over as he discusses the estrangement. "I believe that you have to begin by accepting all bishops as validly ordained. They were only gagged for wanting to elect their own bishops, something that has had a place in Catholic history."

The famed priest-educator shakes his head as if to shed an unhappy memory. "When I am in Rome at meetings, I hear them discussing 'evangelizing culture,' and I ask them just what they mean. They now speak of recognizing 'values around the world,' but I think of how cultures have been wiped out, as the Aztec and Mayan were, in order to get their gold. We have a long history of destroying other cultures or altering them to follow a Western model. Think of the way the Church treated the high culture in India; they made them change their names to things like 'Theophilus' and so on."

He shakes his head again, speaks intensely. "The Catholic Church must transcend its European origins. Pope John Paul is good on that. He speaks of the Church as 'everything that is humanizing.' He sees the values in other cultures. But when others speak of 'evangelizing cultures,' what do they mean? Do they want to accept them or wipe them out? This is the great opportunity to become a truly universal Church, and that is increasingly true of the hierarchy. I was at St. Peter's when the first black bishop was consecrated by Pope Pius XI over forty years ago. Now eighty percent of the African hierarchy is black. We have seen, thanks to John XXIII and Paul VI, the internationalization of the college of cardinals. Pope John Paul II would never have been elected had those men, against great opposition, not broken the European stranglehold on the cardinalate. The universalization of the Church—its expressing itself in cultures other than European—is an inexorable process."

Hesburgh leans back. "Rahner once spoke of the possibility of the pope's moving out of Rome. He said that he might have good reasons to do so. He was getting at this same idea. The Church is not just its Roman heritage. What do you think would happen if, while the pope was on a pilgrimage to Australia, the northern hemisphere was devastated by nuclear war? Would he go back and rebuild Rome just as it had been . . . ?" He lets his rhetorical question hang in the air as he finally takes a sip of coffee.

"Those who criticize today's bishops, and who long for the past, are really talking about a relatively brief cultural period. The smart money is on what is already happening, on this much more variegated Church that is coming into being. That *is* the future. I'm not talking about what is happening on the edges of this process, the mistakes or excesses that can upset so many people. The Church is now a much more comfortable place to be, even if it is a little more untidy. The critics should remember that these eddies along the periphery are not the main stream. The critics are trying to recapture another day when the naked exercise of power solved every difficulty. What is it that they say of the Bourbons? They don't learn anything and they don't forget anything. That exercise of raw power simply won't wash anymore.

"I think," he says, lowering his cup, "that it is possible that there could be a cultural change in the United States through our present bishops. Take a look at their pastoral letter on nuclear war. It's much better than the letters written by the French and the West German bishops." He speaks admiringly, a good judge of people who know what they are doing. "The American letter is written from the perspective of a superpower, not from the viewpoint of small powers that are trying to conjure themselves up as great now on the memories of their past histories. The American bishops are doing something that others cannot do. They wrote the best of the pastoral letters on the subject, the toughest in a way, because it was the first letter that hits everybody. In their letter the French practically endorsed their national policy, but the Americans *questioned* U.S. policy on one of the most important issues of the age.

"Now they are examining the economy, and that hits the pocketbook. That will get everybody's attention too. The fact is that already there has been an enormous amount of discussion on this pastoral letter in draft form. These seminars and exchanges of ideas —we've had a number of them here at Notre Dame —they're all to the good. For example, Ed Hennessy, head of the Allied Corporation, told me of a meeting between a number of Catholic chief executive officers and Archbishop Weakland and Cardinal Bernardin at

Morristown, New Jersey. There was a good deal of disagreement but they talked with each other. *That's* the story, that they talked, not that they disagreed. The businessmen came away from there with greater respect for the bishops and the process they are following. And that process is going to continue. I'm very interested in what they are going to say about women in another letter they have in preparation. I would very much like to see the bishops do something about education. There are many elements that would like to cut back our freedoms. I'm reminded of the University of Paris, founded at the beginning of the thirteenth century. It needed to be liberated from both the Church and civil authorities in Paris. As a result, it got a papal charter which is probably the origin of Pontifical universities, or academic freedom in universities. That is a tradition that must be held onto today when universities are under all kinds of pressure from both the Church and State authorities. Intellectual freedom and responsibility are the very life of universities. I am concerned about efforts to hamstring us Americans from across the ocean." Hesburgh, rich in wisdom about Rome's bureaucratic strategies, smiles confidently. "But I don't worry as long as the collegial process followed by the American bishops is in place."

The much-honored Hesburgh (he recently received his one hundredth honorary degree, a *Guiness Book* record) shifts to some of the specific criticisms that have been leveled against the American bishops.

"They are sometimes cited for supposedly not emphasizing individual virtue as they involve themselves in the morality of social issues. Look, last night in Chicago I spoke to the Council on Foreign Relations about the dangers of nuclear war, a social issue, perhaps the quintessential moral problem of our time. It is not only concerned with the commandment 'Thou shalt not kill,' we're faced with the possibility of reversing the work of creation. While I was talking about social policy, I was emphasizing *hope,* something you don't often hear of. I remember when we presented documents from our discussions at Vienna on this issue to the pope, he reminded everyone of something most had not adverted to, the virtue of hope. As we eventually got rid of slavery, so I think we can eventually rid ourselves of this terrible scourge. Think of the title Freeman Dyson chose for his book on the dangers of nuclear war, *Weapons and Hope.* Hope isn't just a disposition or wishful thinking, it's a virtue that we have to practice, a theological virtue."

Hesburgh gestures emphatically with both hands, like a priest above the bread and wine. "You cannot separate the virtue hope from the social issue. It is implicit in working for this purpose. Peace, as Pope Paul said, is the work of justice. It is a high act of religion to join working for a social cause with virtue and then celebrating it with a Mass, as our students do after they have been out working among those less fortunate than they. Only if you see the relationship between working for a better world and the pursuit of virtue can you understand the meaning of religion. When you get people to live and serve others together, then the Mass means something. We're past those years in which we fulfilled our religious obligations if we 'got Mass *in.*' That's what the bishops are talking about and doing. The Church looks for us to integrate our faith into our lives and our service of others. That is the *holy* and *living* sacrifice that is acceptable to God. That is the meaning of religion, to give ourselves to God as God gives Himself to us. That's how you bind your life together, that is what it means to be virtuous. And I think that is what our modern bishops are calling us as the Church to do."

The university leader has also heard criticisms of Joseph Cardinal Bernardin's call for a consistent ethic of life, a "seamless garment" that relates all the issues affecting the sacredness and dignity of life together. Hesburgh addresses the question like a hitter who has been waiting for just the right pitch. "It is meaningless to be pro-life and pro-MX missiles at the same time. That is exactly what President Reagan does when he calls the MX 'the peacemaker.' This whole consistency question can be seen much better if you look at the inconsistency of those who are pro-life and pro-bargaining-chip nuclear missile. You have the chips but no bargain, and no moral consistency either.

"I think that Cardinal Bernardin is exactly right in calling for a consistent life ethic. Nothing else makes sense. One of the greatest dangers of our day is the emphasis on single issues. The single-issue outlook is a form of myopia in which people get great satisfaction about doing something about something that doesn't touch *them* at all. That is the kind of single-mindedness that Monsignor Ronald Knox wrote about in his famous book *Enthusiasm*. He wrote of the people who were so myopic in their view of Christianity that they thought *they* were the only ones who knew the way to salvation. They are totally blind as a result to every other issue. That's very different from the broad, consistent view of life that you find in Catholic writers like G. K. Chesterton and Rosemary Haughton.

"One issue is never the end-all and be-all of everything. I can give a tight speech on nuclear war and somebody will ask me why I didn't mention abortion. There *are* other things to talk about and there should be a consistency in our viewpoint on all issues that touch on life, whether it's a question of human rights in Salvador, the green revolution that will feed people, or whatever it is. To be consistently in favor of the sacredness and dignity of human life, *that* is the "seamless garment," and I strongly support it. We should remember the poet Horace who spoke of *integer vitae*, the wholeness of life. It is important to remember that only a *whole* person is predictable. That is what the consistent ethic of life urges us to be, whole persons."

Father Hesburgh takes the check from the waitress but remains absorbed with the issues he has been discussing. "Hope *is* a much neglected virtue. The bishops are trying to renew our hope, to help people realize that they can make a difference in what happens in the world. I'm very hopeful about this new Church. I don't have any bad feelings about it at all." The restaurant is empty as we rise to go. "God may be telling Europe that they are not the focus of all things. I feel sorry for some of them. They speak of being Catholic countries, but few people go to Mass, few people let their religion touch their public lives. They seem to have tired blood, and the center of gravity is shifting away from them. They seem to have given up hope."

We walk the length of the restaurant, and Father Hesburgh pauses. "Religion has got to be more than big events, as when Billy Graham gives a talk, or the pope makes a visit, and then everybody goes back to their lives again. How much is changed? What of a country like Venezuela, where millions of people came out to cheer the pope? Half the kids are illegitimate because the people cannot even afford to get married. Four hundred years a Catholic country and they have to import half their clergy. Maybe they are all looking for hope. And that is what I think the new bishops and the new Church here can give the world."

Father Hesburgh stands outlined against the restaurant windows. Beyond them students can be seen on the golf course, which is struggling to turn green. It is, a visitor recalls, the first day of spring, a good day to hear somebody speak about hope.

EIGHT

A NEIGHBOR
TO EVERY
OTHER PERSON
ON OUR GLOBE

THE BISHOPS' MEETING,
COLLEGEVILLE, MINNESOTA, JUNE 1985

A SLAB of concrete a hundred feet across rises like a
sail above the rolling green sea of hills ninety miles
northwest of Minneapolis. It holds the tumbling bells
of St. John's Abbey and University of Collegeville, a
Benedictine institution that has been a center for monastic life and education for more than a century.
America's Catholic bishops gather here in mid-June of
1985 to pray, reflect, and discuss an agenda that includes their critical proposals for the second draft of
their pastoral letter on the American economy. They
assemble in the old gym, a spacious steel raftered hall
whose basketball floor has been covered with canvas
and set with round tables for the small group discussions that are to precede their general comments on

the letter in progress. The mood is relaxed, perhaps because half the Catholic churches in the country started in converted gymnasiums with mass regularly offered beneath folded backboards and silent game clocks. It is as much a reminder of Catholicism's beginnings as the abbey which played such an important role in educating its immigrant community. Some of the bishops dress informally and selected priests and laypeople join them in their conversations about the document.

On an elevated platform along the far wall sit the officers of the National Conference of Bishops, James Malone, bishop of Youngstown, Ohio, its president; John May, archbishop of St. Louis, vice president; and the boyish looking Monsignor Daniel Hoye, the general secretary who, as a veteran observer says, "is the only outsider in the hall who is sure to be a bishop." They sit beneath a literal old rugged cross that stands against panels of colored cloth. As Malone welcomes the bishops who have been ordained and also remembers those who have died since their last meeting, former United States Senator Eugene McCarthy, an alumnus of St. John's College, surveys them from the side of the entrance. Silver haired, a strong hint of F.D.R. in his robust good looks and jauntiness, he symbolizes the interest that the outside world has taken in these church leaders. Since the issuance of the 60,000-word first draft of the pastoral the previous November the bishops have received abundant advice and criticism. It seems not unfitting that as committee chairman Rembert Weakland, archbishop of Milwaukee, is introduced, an electrical storm begins to make a muffled passage across the surrounding prairie.

If noted conservative leader William F. Buckley, Jr., has referred to the bishops' first draft as "so sad an accumulation of lumpen clichés," columnist James Kilpatrick has ridiculed "their gentle notion . . . that all men are, or at least morally ought to be, substantially equal in this world's goods. The reality is that some of God's creatures are more ambitious, more talented, more productive, more industrious and just plain luckier than others." Commentator George Will has accused the bishops of believing that "God subscribes to the liberal agenda," thereby reducing themselves to "just another reedy voice in the capital's chorus, part of Washington's audible wallpaper: always there, never noticed." Former White House communications adviser David Gergen, however, has written that the bishops spoke up "at exactly the right time in the right way at a moment when the nation is about to make crucial economic decisions." The New York *Times,* joining the Philadelphia *Inquirer* in a warm editorial response, called the bishops' draft letter "a plea that America give priority to the human condition." The Washington *Post* welcomed the bishops' demonstration that "the Church's concern for life does not end at birth."

The bishops have become accustomed to denunciations in the *Wall Street Journal* and business magazines, but they have also witnessed a quick marshaling of the widespread forces of the Catholic establishment. The Jesuits, for example, one of the most influential religious groups in American life, quickly endorsed the bishops' aims and began, in the pages of their *National Jesuit News,* to study how the economy pastoral, particularly its emphasis on service to the poor, might apply to their varied ministries. Dozens of Catholic colleges and universities across the country convened symposia to discuss the first draft of the economic pastoral. Typical was that held in January 1985 at the Catholic University of America. Its president, Father William Byron, S.J., a trained economist, examined a wide range of business issues from a moral perspective. These included economic expansion, productivity, welfare dependency, consumer spending, poverty, and mergers and acquisitions. He observed that the proposed pastoral letter rested on the three themes of "human dignity, societal bonds, and the quest for the deeper meaning of economic activity."

Multiplied dozens of times, such meetings indicate the lively state of American Catholicism and reflect its capacity for almost instant feedback to the bishops on serious matters. It also suggests the rapid manner in which Catholic Church leaders can seed the consciousness of their people with pastoral concerns and elicit a variety of responses, not excluding sharp dissents, that exemplify both pragmatic collegiality and practical organizational communication. The intricate wiring of Catholic life—schools, parishes, universities, newspapers, magazines, journals, even a television network—became the transmitter of the debate about the bishops' letter. "I.B.M.," one university professor observed, "would like to be able to do as well."

The business world seemed as irritated in general as some of its individual members were fascinated in particular by the bishops' bold venture into the realm of capitalism. A great many felt, however, that the bishops should concern themselves with the hereafter and leave the here and now to them. What could the bishops know about business, the free market, the meeting of payroll obligations? As Archbishop Weakland takes his place at the podium he remembers the most recent of the dozens of meetings he has addressed in the last six months. In the heart of Wall Street before 400 business leaders at an ecumenically sponsored symposium held at Pace College he had dealt with the often criticized length of the pastoral, observing that one priest from his own diocese suggested that the bishops should stop sending pastoral letters and start sending pastoral postcards. Weakland defended the main thrust and intention of the bishops' work, noting the intense interest at home and abroad in what the bishops were doing. Why else had these executives come to hear him? "We've hit a nerve," he had said to the businessmen, "there's no doubt about it." He smiles gently as he begins, "My brother bishops, having faced Wall Street, you're easy."

The prelates seem absorbed as Weakland, reviewing the suggestions that had come to his committee not only from the bishops but from Catholic and non-Catholic laypeople, prepares them for the round table discussions that will fill the morning. The bishops have already received a summary report of their own responses to the first draft. Generally favorable, they include suggestions to modify the first draft's length and style, to make its tone more positive, to treat the economy as a whole, to be more specific in recommendations for policy changes, and to offer a rationale for the role of the government in the economy. The respondent bishops also wanted a better articulated relationship to the 1983 peace pastoral, and wanted some discussion of other topics affected by the economy, such as family life.

This morning the process of collegiality, that hallmark of the NCCB, is intensified, raised to a new power through subjecting it to yet a further process. This kind of challenge, however, is borne easily by these dutiful men who, whatever their personal feelings, are accustomed to—indeed, feel comfortable and reassured by—putting their shoulders to such administrative wheels as the concentrated group discussions that are about to begin. Led by facilitator Father Don Bargen, the bishops, divided into small groups, will exchange views on five areas under which the suggestions about the first draft have been classified:

1. *Specificity*. Some respondents feel that a certain level of specificity is essential in this letter to communicate effectively and to have an impact on government policy. Others feel that specific

suggestions could limit the letter's lasting effect, making it seem "dated."

2. *Option for the poor.* While affirming this phrase, controversial even though taken from papal utterances, how can the letter best explain the notion in the context of American culture?

3. *Linkage.* Many bishops have asked for greater emphasis on the linkage between this pastoral letter and the 1983 letter on War and Peace. How can this linkage be best expressed?

4. *Implementation.* Recognizing that many organizations and structures of the Church share responsibility for making the proposals of the present pastoral letter work, what are the most effective means and groups or audiences to reach in the process of implementation?

5. *Separate Message.* Many bishops want the final pastoral draft to be accompanied by a brief "pastoral message" addressed to American Catholics in general in a more inspirational and less technical tone. Do the bishops in general now agree with this suggestion, and, if so, how should it be pursued?

Although nobody mentions it out loud, the purpose of this exercise is to avoid a session of potentially long and unfocussed observations, as hazardous as unprepared sermons, by the members of the conference. It also aims at preventing prominent leaders of the conference from dominating its thinking through speeches which, even made with the best intentions and good will, might have undue influence on the deliberations. This is, then, a process of purification, the moment to plunge the glowing metal they have hammered out on the forge of their first effort into the cool well of reflection and revision. After interim reports at the end of the morning, the discussions will be summarized and for a limited period on the following morning the bishops, through representatives or as individuals, will speak about them from the floor. Archbishop Weakland will then respond on behalf of his committee and turn with its members to the work of preparing a second draft before the November bishops' meeting in Washington, D.C.

The reporters groan, Eugene McCarthy smiles wryly, for this is the dull, almost glazed face of contemporary group dynamics applied to church life. The assembled journalists prefer live discussion with every possibility of disagreement and just the off chance that conflict will emerge to reveal the conservative–progressive divisions they suspect and half hope to uncover among the bishops. The members of the media are disappointed at what Bishop Pierre Dumaine of San Jose, California, will later liken to "covering a pinochle tournament." As the bishops, joined at each table by priest and lay delegates, begin their discussions the reporters seek out interviews with individual prelates, luring them out of the hall for brief question and answer sessions, attempting to knead some drama out of proceedings that are designed to transcend personalities through the mechanics of collegial process. "Deadening but effective," a battle scarred veteran of bishops' meetings, "the true triumph of their bureaucracy."

Younger reporters have heard mostly apocryphal tales of the way bishops' meetings were conducted before they were opened to the press in the early 1970's. They long for some craggy cardinal from central casting to rise to his feet, as the late James Francis McIntyre of Los Angeles sometimes did, to castigate a younger member of the episcopate. The journalists huddle together over coffee convinced that despite the calm of the proceedings a storm is gathering around the American bishops as real as that now enveloping the old building in which they are convened.

They speak of the Brazilian theologian, Father Leonard Boff, who was recently silenced by Roman authorities—forbidden to write, teach, or speak—because of his supposed deviations from orthodoxy in his work in what has come to be known as "Liberation Theology." The perfect of the Sacred Congregation of the Faith, Joseph Cardinal Ratzinger, is rumored to be investigating theologians in many countries, including the United States, pressing them to conform strictly to what he considers orthodox views, especially on such issues as the possibility of ordaining women priests. Pope John Paul II, according to an American bishop who recently visited him, is vehement on this particular question and would eliminate any candidate for the bishopric who has ever entertained even the possibility of a woman's becoming a priest. The pope has also told visiting bishops that they must place orthodox adherence to church teachings as *the* essential quality in any men they might propose as future bishops.

The conversations among the reporters turn to Pope John Paul II's recent strong endorsement of the vigorous, highly secretive Opus Dei society. He has not only granted the group independence from other ecclesiastical authority by giving them what amounts to their own extra-territorial diocese but he has also embraced them in other significant ways. The pope, whose new press secretary is a member of this group, just personally ordained, within a larger group of candidates, twenty-eight of Opus Dei's members to the priesthood. One respected journalist explains that the rectors of the seven ecclesiastical universities in Rome protested the plans of Opus Dei leaders to establish their own university in that city. They presented their petitions through William Cardinal Baum, an American who heads the Roman educational congregation. A few days later the pope told Baum that he had decided to grant the permission against the wishes of the rectors. Cardinal Baum returned to his office to find the Opus Dei superior waiting for him, already informed of the permission. This society is perceived by the reporters as intent on restoring a medieval, devotional Catholicism, rigidly orthodox, blindly loyal to the pope, standing with him in his seeming self-perception as a messianic figure confronting the new barbarians.

Yet another respected religion writer suggests that the special Synod of Bishops scheduled for November 1985 may be the most important story of the year. There is speculation that the pope intends to use it not so much to validate the advances of Vatican II, whose spirit it is scheduled to commemorate, but to trim them back severely. Other writers disagree, joining their own rumors and stories to the free flow of the discussion, as delicious to their restless, curious minds in some ways as in others it is improbable. The American Catholic Church, one of them says, is too powerful, too rich ironically enough, to be pushed around by the Vatican. Brazil, on the other hand, is so poor that despite its huge Catholic population, its 300 bishops, and its progressive cardinals, it can be ignored. Evaristo Cardinal Arns, archbishop of São Paulo, the largest Catholic diocese in the world, has recently traveled throughout the United States with stories of Roman curial snooping and interference in the Brazilian church. The silenced Father Boff, he tells people, is his protege and although the theologian has accepted his punishment loyally, Cardinal Ratzinger now seems to toy with him by making the term of his discipline somewhat indeterminate. Rome does not even answer the letters sent by the president of the Brazilian bishops' conference, Bishop Jose Ivo Lorscheiter, and Brazilians must read news of their church in the Italian papers. Such control could never be exercised over Americans, the reporters agree, but they do not doubt current Roman efforts to tighten up and to diminish the stature and influence of the very bishops who are busily conferring at tables just beyond them.

These melancholy discussions are counterpointed with some humor as Richard Cowden, correspondent for the *Wanderer,* the St. Paul based paper that has been so severely critical of the American bishops, announces to Tom Fox, editor of the liberal *National Catholic Reporter,* "I come here as your enemy." He accuses Fox and his paper of being guilty of the Aryan heresy, tells another writer he encounters that "I plan to condemn you too but I won't get around to it for some time yet. My principal targets are Archbishop Weakland of Milwaukee and Archbishop Peter Gerety of Newark. Then I would like to have Teilhard de Chardin's body exhumed and thrown into the Hudson River." The bemused chuckles of the writers do not cover their uneasiness about such intentions, they speak of ultra-conservative groups, most of them small in comparison to their letter-writing influence in Rome, who feel that the present American bishops are, through exercises such as composing this pastoral letter, destroying the church.

What the journalists know for a fact is that Joseph Cardinal Ratzinger has been severely critical of the post-Vatican II Church, seeing it as "self-destructive." His recent interviews, just collected in a book entitled *Report on The Faith,* also take issue with specific aspects of American Catholic life. Ratzinger continues to insist that American theologians do not challenge the values of their culture but rather accept them in their work, thus blurring the distinction between good and evil. He also contends that "a certain feminist mentality" has infected American women's religious communities, including among their excesses, "the discovery of professionalism," and "the entrance, sometimes without any filtering, of psychology and psychoanalysis in every convent school." What some people call the "spirit of the council" Ratzinger sees as an anti-spirit that has done grave harm to religion through its excessive openness to the secular world.

The German cardinal has also continued to criticize national conferences of bishops, declaring that a national conference such as the one whose members are spread so diligently at the tables in the storm clouded gym, "should remain essentially an instrument of service, without being weighted down organizationally . . . a limited structure, without a juridical dimension, orders of the day and the creation of offices." Although in remarks made on June 9, less than a week before this meeting opened, he stressed his views were his own and defended dissent in the Church, Ratzinger has left little doubt about his present feelings about national conferences of bishops. His main argument is a brilliantly clear echo of that used by curial opponents against the National Catholic Welfare Council in 1922. The conferences must be limited, Ratzinger insists, "to defend the flexibility and the weight of the personal responsibility of the local bishop."

The reporters sip their coffee, gesture toward the

bishops huddled in serious conversations across the hall. "These bishops," one of them says, "handle Roman criticism like Ratzinger's not by responding directly but by continuing to do what they're doing now. They just keep on working together." Another observes that "The present leadership is very strong, with cardinals like Bernardin and O'Connor, and archbishops like Weakland and John Quinn of San Francisco. The question of the future, however, is something like that of the Supreme Court. The pope will make all the appointments of bishops for the next several years. Will he change the character of this group from mildly progressive orthodoxy to absolute conservatism?" The journalists agree that the present cohort of bishops is led by men who understand the proportional importance of national conferences, that they do not exaggerate their authority or see it in any way as a challenge to Rome. They hold to their view that conferences come from an ecumenical church council and are rooted in the ancient theological principle of collegiality. They are not, then, dangerous democratic improvisations of recent origin. National episcopal conferences possess theological credentials that cannot easily be stamped invalid by any critic, no matter how highly placed he may be in the Roman power structure. "These bishops make their stand through their functioning as a conference more than through debating their own right to exist," one of the writers concludes, "and they will not roll over and play dead for Cardinal Ratzinger."

The latter, one journalist says grimly, "is considered to be one of the pope's principal advisers. He may be speaking for him even when he says he's only speaking for himself." Another reporter who has just joined the conversation good-naturedly disagrees, "Oh, I don't know, I hear they don't really hit it off. Something about the strain of one being Polish and the other German." Laughter follows as the reporters, sensing that the bishops are about to take a break, pick up their notebooks and move into positions to button-hole specific prelates for comments or interviews as soon as they leave their tables.

The journalists have grown to like and respect, with very few exceptions, these American bishops. They work to maintain professional objectivity in reporting on the prelates' activities but in their hearts they seem to be rooting for them. They are covering, however, not just the interesting or winning private personalities of bishops but, more significantly, what the bishops become when joined together in collegial process. This is not the U.S. Senate with its bluff and open negotiating, nor the British parliament with its charming and eccentric traditions. This is a different kind of convocation and its real power is a function of the way its serious and dutiful members have learned to work together. They constitute a third entity as they assume the obligations of the process that is such a central ingredient of their operation. The concept of a collegial cooperative body envisioned by John Cardinal Dearden a generation ago purposely lacks dramatic flair; their rejection of rending their

garments and histrionic prophesying allows the bishops to draw on their strengths as administrators and
their instincts as pastors. Their process frees them to
be themselves and to use their most highly polished
skills at the same time. In this diligent but dull application of the bishops' attention and good will,
Dearden's hopes may be observed in full and vigorous
bloom.

As his committee sifts the day's comments on Friday
evening Archbishop Weakland remembers the criticism he has heard during the long season since the first
draft of the letter was presented. Some people have
wanted to divide it into two letters, others to digest
it, still others have concentrated on eliminating whatever might make it seem a partisan political document. He realizes that the committee members' early
decision not to explore capitalism theoretically has
limited their analysis, as one observer put it, to the
effects of that system rather than the system itself. At
the very core of many bishops' concern is the letter's
commitment to Pope Paul VI's theme of a "preferential option for the poor." Although repeated and explained by Pope John Paul II, this phrase can be easily
misunderstood. Forged into a slogan, it has the potential of confusing if not alienating many Catholics.
Archbishop Frank Hurley of Anchorage, Alaska, had
raised the point in a brief roundup of comments from
the floor that morning. "The phrase 'preferential option for the poor,'" he reminded his colleagues,

"comes out of Latin America where there are only two classes, rich and poor. To use it in reference to American middle-class people is to risk polarizing them. The middle class is the mainstay of the Catholic Church in this country."

Weakland has thought long and hard about shortening the pastoral letter. He would need a budget committee on words, he thinks with an inner smile, to do that effectively. The main concerns of his brother bishops are indeed familiar to him: be specific enough, but not too specific; let the bishops speak as moral teachers rather than as economic technicians; link the economic pastoral with the peace pastoral so that the unity—what is called the "seamless garment" —of Catholic teaching will be apparent; plan the implementation phase well so that the impact of the letter will be as broad and deep as possible within the church as well as in the general culture. He reviews these issues as the bishops convene on Saturday morning. The tornado and severe thunderstorm alerts that had been sounded across the Minnesota farmland the night before have been called off. It promises to be a sunny day.

"The feedback," he explains to the attentive bishops, "has been quite helpful." He reviews their concerns in detail, indicating how the committee will attempt to incorporate their suggestions into the pastoral's second draft. Mindful of their charge to write a letter that will be truly pastoral in helping people from their consciences while also adding to the public

debate on the moral dimensions of economic problems, the committee will attempt to give better de-
scriptions of individual economic and social problems
and be more careful and nuanced in suggesting solutions. "One cannot just talk about a plant closing as
a moral issue without being specific," Weakland says,
"We cannot talk about poverty without discussing
the feminization of poverty. It may be, as some suggest, that we should pose these concerns in question
form or that we should offer multiple choice solutions. Above all we want to show these issues specifically within a moral rather than a political context."

In an easy, confident manner the Milwaukee archbishop summarizes the bishops' concerns about questions as diverse as the letter's definition of poverty and
its recommendations about the World Bank's loans to
the poorest countries. He explores the phrase "preferential option for the poor" as he had at a news conference the previous day, reminding his audience of Pope
John Paul II's explanatory words, already cited in
paragraph 53 of the first draft. During a visit to Puebla, Mexico, the pope had described this option as "a
call to have a special openness with the poor and the
weak, those that suffer and weep, those that are humiliated and left on the margin of society, so as to help
them win their dignity as human persons and children
of God." The bishops do not want to lose the powerful resonance of the phrase because it seems to catch
their spirit and motivation in writing this document.
Still it is a delicate phrase and they want to "build

bridges," not burn them. They certainly do not want the term to degenerate into an all-purpose slogan. "We are asked," Weakland says reflectively, "to have an openness *with* not just *to* the poor. That means the poor cannot be considered just objects of charity and," he concludes, "it also implies action."

He next explores his colleagues' desire to link the present pastoral letter to their 1983 peace letter. The archbishop's smile reveals the dilemma of a chairman who wants to acknowledge everybody's observations. "They want to do this but not enlarge the document, and they want it done in a natural and not a forced way." Yes, he nods, as if to say, "We will do our best." He conveys the same sense about the "militarization" of the American economy through its heavy dependence on defense and associated industries. Weakland turns to the many challenges associated with the implementation of the pastoral letter once it is finally issued some time in 1986. "It must be implemented within the church," he notes, "as the whole People of God, and we must use all our educational programs to teach and to keep ourselves constantly aware of our problem. There will be obstacles that will come from pressures of the culture." The bishops are familiar but apparently unfazed by these and the committee chairman moves on to another area about which there is great concern. "We bishops must ask ourselves how it affects *us* and *our* life-style. This applies to priests and seminarians as well. We are not just talking to corporate executives." He alludes to the oft-raised question of the church as an economic actor: an employer of thousands of people, a steward of gifts and finances, an entity as much in need of serious self-examination as any other on the economic scene.

After reviewing the means, including cooperative efforts with other episcopal conferences, that have been suggested for the implementation process the committee chairman concludes with some observations about the separate non-technical message that will accompany the full text of the forthcoming letter, "We want to stress the gospel themes that lead to conversion of heart," Weakland says, "and we wish to stay on a high level as we highlight the issues that are discussed in the letter itself. There is some conflict," he says dryly, "about the size of this accompanying document. Suggestions range from one to ten pages." He smiles again, "Let the committee try."

The archbishop conveys a sense of comfort. He feels a firm ground of support from the body of the bishops, a ratifying kind of encouragement for the work of his committee. Its members are doing what the bishops want and most of the latter group's comments aim at improving the letter rather than in any way disturbing its essential character. Weakland tests out his perceptions of the bishops' feelings. "You don't want us to water down the first document and you feel that the biblical section is very good. The ethical section is good but it is tough going. As to the application, you seem to say 'Yes, but be careful, we don't want to have a political letter." Weakland turns away from the microphone, reassured by the mood of the hall that he has accurately caught the pastoral intentions of his brother bishops.

The bishops, some reporting for the members of their discussion groups and others speaking on their own, quickly validate the growing impression that these prelates stand strongly together on the fundamentals of the letter on the economy. "I just wish," John Cardinal O'Connor, who as archbishop of New York is Wall Street's pastor, says in a brief interview with the New York *Times,* "I just wish that the business community and the economic community could be here. They'd be relieved to see the integrity of the process." Weakland will say later in the day that his committee's project got a "new lift" from the day's positive comments by the bishops.

The bishops who speak echo many of the concerns already identified by Weakland, including the manner in which the phrase "preferential option for the poor" is to be interpreted. They clearly do not want to create unnecessary and unjustified divisions within the Catholic community, they do not want middle class Catholics and others to feel alienated by some misapplication of this phrase. Still, they want to retain it in the document. Archbishop Patrick Flores of San Antonio reminds his confreres that "in building bridges we have to be on both sides of the river. The poor do not see us as *with* them." He pauses, noting a sad pastoral reality in his own experience, "And some well-to-do Catholics say that bishops who work with the poor are communists." Bishop Joseph Sullivan, an auxiliary bishop of Brooklyn, endorses the option for the poor in order to challenge the Church about its calling in a country that is being turned into a two-class society by government policy. The bishops' desires not to cause misunderstandings for their middle-class parishoners must, as they see it, be blended with a true expression of their concern for poverty in all its forms.

A related concern surfaces as one bishop observes that some feel that the document, in a country where there is a tendency to equate capitalism with religion, is not "shocking" enough. Can the principles of Catholic social teaching, this spokesman asks, be "incorporated into our system without seriously damaging the system which we claim to be the freest? Or does the U.S. system require substantial change to bring about social justice?" The bishops apparently want such potentially disturbing questions raised even as they also wish to endorse the strong and healthy aspects of the American economy.

Other bishops want the letter to emphasize the eternal destiny of the human person as something transcending material fulfillment in the secular order of the economy. Still others, including Bishops Roger Mahony of Stockton, California, and Maurice Dingman of Des Moines, Iowa, speak of the newly developed chapter on food and agriculture, defending the economic rights of farm workers and the value of individual farm ownership in the age of corporate agriculture. Archbishop Peter Gerety of Newark counterpoints this with a moving reflection on the desolation to be found in so many big cities, often caused by suburban growth financed by tax breaks. What will happen, he asks, to metropolitan areas that gave meaning to the word "urbanity"?

Over and over the prelates express, with slightly different emphases, the major critical themes that have already been identified by Archbishop Weakland. But their overwhelming support for the developing letter is unmistakable. Bishop Michael Murphy of Erie, Pennsylvania, sums up their feelings by saying to the committee, "Right on. Tighten up. Don't back off."

Weakland glances down at his notes as he takes the podium once more. "It is clear," he begins slowly, "that we want to make this document an invitation to greater moral responsibility about the issues it discusses. I think that if we examine some of the European criticism of the ethics section (he refers to comments in the Italian popular Catholic magazine *Il Regno*) where they seem to think that it is all a closed book. Actually, Catholic social teaching, as we mention, is a growing body of teaching that is open-ended rather than closed." His tone is reassuring, non-defensive, he wants to provide the bishops with the setting for the committee's work. "They don't want to improvise, they want to play from a score," the archbishop musician says in summing up his colleagues' concern that they have adequate supportive information about the letter's main points.

Weakland quickly reviews a number of associated concerns. The nature of the letter's teaching authority has been questioned. He refers to the introduction to the second part of the first draft, paragraphs he would like to switch to the very beginning of its next version. They are taken from the 1983 letter, *The Challenge of Peace:* ". . . not every statement in this letter has the same moral authority. At times we reassert universally binding moral principles. At still other times we reaffirm statements of recent popes and the teaching of Vatican II. Again, at other times we apply moral principles to specific cases. While making applications we realize—and we wish readers to realize —that prudential judgments are involved based on specific circumstances which can change or which can be interpreted differently by people of good will. However, the moral judgments that we make in specific cases, while not binding in conscience, are to be given serious attention and consideration by Catholics as they determine whether their moral judgments are consistent with the Gospel."

The archbishop acknowledges the comments about the newly developed chapter on food and agriculture, noting that the need to focus on the short term crisis of the small farmer does not mean that long range concerns do not also exist. He turns to the frequently raised issue of the need for an analysis of capitalistic theory. "Marxism," he observes, "has a consistent line of theory but capitalism does not. Were we to deal theoretically with capitalism we would have to cover everybody on the spectrum between John Kenneth

Galbraith and Milton Friedman. If we tried to do that, the letter would go all over the lot."

The committee chairman, ordinarily monastically calm, becomes passionate as he speaks of placing the idea of the common good against the overworked justifying imperatives of rugged individualism. Indeed, he has lectured repeatedly on this theme, citing the thought of the interdependent common good first spoken of by Pope John XXIII in the early sixties. "If you bring this up," he says, "you will be criticized as advocating 'statism.'" Weakland has reached the core of the motivation that he has felt deeply in the years he has spent working on this project. He is close to the deepest feelings of many of the bishops as well. Capitalism has much to recommend it but it is hardly without faults. "John Stuart Mill and Adam Smith spoke of the efficiency of the capitalistic system," Weakland says, "They recognized, however, that the distribution of wealth was not built into the system. They reasoned that other values and forces in society would have to take care of that important question of equity." The assembled bishops rivet their attention on the man to whom they have entrusted the responsibility of authoring the kind of pastoral letter they want. "We must be aware of the human costs that accompanied the Industrial Revolution. They were tremendous and we cannot ignore them when we speak of capitalism's glories. We believe that many of the human costs that characterize moments of change in the capitalist system can be reduced by clear objectives and by learning from history." That, the bishops sense, is precisely why they have undertaken the writing of this letter. Weakland concludes, "If we go too far into capitalistic theory, this document won't be pastoral in nature." Prolonged applause follows, a settled, steady sound that is an unequivocal signal of the bishops' approval of the manner in which Weakland has carried out his task.

Later, standing in the sunlight outside the abbey chapel, Weakland reflects on his experience. He understands the work that lies ahead but now, in a way that is clearly different from the uncertainty that pervaded the meeting the previous November, he feels sure of his direction, confident of the Catholic social teachings that are the backbone of the letter. He knows there is a danger of pastoral "burn-out," of loading the Catholic community with too many demanding letters in too short a time. He is also aware of the time pressures, of the critics, both lay and Catholic, who have launched not only theoretical but personal attacks on the bishops for their work. More of that can be expected. The *Wall Street Journal* had printed a brief, chiding editorial yesterday. There are weeks and months of work ahead but Weakland seems, if anything, more peaceful than ever about these challenges. He seems to be speaking for many bishops when he answers a question about the ultimate objective of preparing this pastoral letter.

"This work has been a real grace for me," he says slowly, "a challenge, and a delight in working with so many people who have been a great source of enrichment. I've traveled so much they're beginning to introduce me as the archbishop *from* Milwaukee instead of the archbishop *of* Milwaukee." He grins, becomes thoughtful. "I think, however, that even in my own diocese it brings a greater dimension, greater ecclesial life to the church there. It develops a greater sense of being Catholic and of relationship to the whole society." He pauses. "I think the real objective of writing a pastoral letter on the economy is to help everybody understand what it means to be a neighbor to every other person on this globe."

APPENDIX:

SELECTIONS FROM THE FIRST DRAFT
OF THE U.S. BISHOPS' PASTORAL LETTER
ON CATHOLIC SOCIAL TEACHING AND
THE U.S. ECONOMY

INTRODUCTION
THE CHURCH AND THE ECONOMY:
WHY WE SPEAK

Every perspective on economic life that is human, moral and Christian must be shaped by two questions: What does the economy do *for* people? What does it do *to* people? It is concern for the effects of the U.S. economy on the lives of millions of human beings that leads us to issue this pastoral letter.

In the Pastoral Constitution on the Church in the Modern World the Second Vatican Council declared that "the joys and hopes, the griefs and anxieties of the people of this age, especially those who are poor or in any way afflicted, these too are the joys and hopes, the griefs and anxieties of the followers of Christ."[1] The joy and suffering of living people shape our commitments and guide our conclusions throughout this letter. The ministry of the church has given it firsthand knowledge of the hopes and struggles of many groups and classes of people, both in this country and throughout the world. We know the patience, the happiness and the worry of men and women who live modestly but fear for their future. We preach and bring the sacraments to many in our church who have benefited greatly from the wealth of this nation. We see their desire to do good and their courage in seeking to do it. We know the joy and the anguish of those who struggle just to survive, living and dying in poverty. All of these men, women and children are our people because they are God's people.

The poor have a special claim on our concern because they are vulnerable and needy. We believe that all—Christians, Jews, those of other faiths or no faith at all—must measure their actions and choices by what they do *for* and *to* the poor. As pastors and as citizens we are convinced of one fundamental criterion for economic decisions, policies and institutions: They must all be at the service of human beings. The economy was made for people, *all* people, and not the other way around.

. . .

In this effort to discern the signs of the times in U.S. economic life we have listened to many ways of analyzing the problems and many proposed solutions. In our discussion, study and reflection one thing has become evident. There is no clear consensus about the nature of the problems facing the country or about the best ways to address these problems effectively. The nation wonders whether it faces fundamentally new economic challenges that call for major changes in its way of doing business or whether adjustments within the framework of existing institutions will suffice. Public opinion polls and daily press reports fluctuate between optimism and pessimism over the future, whether national or global.

This uncertainty and alternation between hope and apprehension has many causes. The U.S. economy has been immensely successful in providing for the material needs and in raising the living standard of its citizens. Our nation is one of the richest on earth. Despite this great wealth the country has recently gone through a severe recession with the highest unemployment rates since the Great Depression of the 1930s. In the recovery from this painful period the situation has improved, but very serious doubts remain about the future. The rate of poverty has risen sharply in recent years and is now at the highest level since 1965. Unemployment is exceptionally high even in the midst of the recovery, especially for minorities and youth. Some regions have been especially hard hit and their economic futures are in doubt. Farmers with moderate-sized holdings, workers in aging heavy industries, owners of vulnerable small businesses, and the poor and minority population in many central cities are often tempted to despair.

Some analysts argue that these problems result from a fundamental structural transition in the U.S. economy, caused by new international competition, the movement of labor-intensive industries out of the country, the displacement of jobs by advanced technology and a shift from a manufacturing and industrial economy to a service economy with lower-paying jobs. Add to this a major threat to the stability of the international financial system posed by the huge debts of several developing countries. A deepening crisis would leave no one untouched.

. . .

The investment of human creativity and material resources in the production of the weapons of war only makes these economic problems more intractable. The rivalry and mutual fear between the superpowers channel resources away from the task of creating a more just and productive economy into a seemingly endless effort to create more powerful and technologically sophisticated weaponry. The East-West arms race, on both the conventional and nuclear levels, is a threat to world peace and a threat to economic justice as well. It drains financial resources that should be dedicated to meeting human needs; diverts many excellent minds from projects that serve life and create new jobs into projects that threaten death and create weapons that are virtually unusable.

Even more damaging from the viewpoint of economic justice are the arms races between developing countries and their neighbors. Poor countries can ill afford to use their scarce resources to buy weapons when they lack food, education and health care for large parts of their population. The willingness of the superpowers and other developed countries to fan the flames of arms competition among many developing countries poses another serious threat to global economic justice.

Economic criteria cannot be the sole determinants of military and arms policies. But it is clear that one of the signs of our times is the growing militarization of the U.S. and global economies. As Pope John Paul II said during his recent visit to Canada, "the arms race is a real threat of death . . . while its economic cost deprives so many countries of the effective means for their development."[2] Discussion of unmet economic problems, therefore, is inextricably bound to efforts to reduce military conflict and rivalry. The link between justice and peace and the opposition between guns and butter are vividly exemplified in our own time.

One thing is certain in all this discussion: The stakes are enormously high. U.S. economic institutions and policies directly affect the dignity and well-being of millions of U.S. citizens. Choices made here have worldwide effects. Decisions made abroad have immediate consequences in the lives of U.S. citizens. How our country responds to the economic problems it faces will help or harm people all around the globe.

. . .

In this letter we seek to support human dignity, strengthen the bonds of life in society and uncover the deeper meaning of the many activities that form economic life. These themes are the basis of the perspectives and recommendations proposed in this letter.

We write with two purposes. The first is to provide

guidance for members of our own church as they seek to form their consciences and reach moral decisions about economic matters. The second is to add our voice to the public debate about U.S. economic policies. In pursuing the first of these purposes we argue from a distinctively Christian perspective that has been shaped by the Bible and by the content of Christian tradition, and from a standpoint that reflects our faith in God: Father, Son and Holy Spirit. The second purpose demands that our arguments be developed in a reasoned manner that will be persuasive to those who do not share our faith or our tradition.

. . .

In addition, our perspective and our conclusions are shaped by an overriding concern for the impact of decisions and policies on the lives of people, especially the poor. *Our fundamental norm is this: Will this decision or policy help the poor and deprived members of the human community and enable them to become more active participants in economic life?*

PART ONE

BIBLICAL AND THEOLOGICAL

FOUNDATIONS

I. THE CHRISTIAN VISION OF ECONOMIC LIFE

The basis for all that the church believes about the moral dimensions of economic life is its vision of the

transcendent worth—the sacredness—of human beings. *The dignity of the human person, realized in community with others, is the criterion against which all
aspects of economic life must be measured.*

．　．　．

Human personhood must be respected with a reverence that is religious. When we deal with each other
we should do so with the sense of awe that arises in
the presence of something holy and sacred. For that
is what human beings are: We are created "in the
image and likeness of God."[1] This dignity is all the
more evident to Christians when we consider the
destiny of union and friendship with God opened up
for us by the redeeming love of Jesus Christ to which
all people without exception are called.[2] Economic
life must serve and support this dignity which needs
to be realized in relationship and solidarity with others. To be human is to hear the call to community.
We can find true identity only "through a sincere
gift" of ourselves.[3] Human wisdom and experience
confirm this religious conviction that human life is
essentially communitarian.

These convictions have a biblical and theological
basis. They also draw support from a long tradition
of philosophical reflection and from the common
human experience of contemporary men and
women. Our discussion of U.S. economic life today
is rooted in this vision of human dignity and social
solidarity, and so we want to begin by developing
this vision more fully in biblical and theological
terms.

A. Biblical Perspectives on Economic Life

For Christians the Scriptures are the prime source for our understanding of God's goodness to us and of our corresponding responsibility to God and our neighbors. The Scriptures contain many passages that speak directly of economic life. But we must also attend carefully to the Bible's deeper vision of God, of human personhood and of life in society. Although the Bible does not and cannot give us simple and direct answers to today's complex economic questions, it can and must shape our vision of the meaning of economic life. We Christians claim the Hebrew Scriptures as a common sacred heritage with our Jewish brothers and sisters, and therefore we wish to join with them in seeking an economic life worthy of the divine revelation we share. Moreover both the Old and New Testaments have shaped our cultural heritage, and biblical images exercise a powerful and persuasive influence for good on our national political imagination. The biblical challenge is important to the whole of this letter. It is a challenge to faith, a challenge to the churches and a challenge to our culture.

1. Creation, Covenant and Community

The most fundamental conviction of our faith is that human life is fulfilled in the knowledge and love of the living God, in communion with others who are called to love the same God and who are themselves recipients of God's love. We know this goal and

challenge through the gift of God's own self-disclo-
sure in word and deed. The Sacred Scriptures, written
under the inspiration of the Holy Spirit and interpreted by the church with the assistance of this same
Spirit, record God's guidance and direction so that
men and women may enter into full communion with
him and with each other, and witness to God's saving
deeds. In these Scriptures we discover a God who is
creator of heaven and earth, who does not abandon
sinners and who enters into a covenant with a people
and forms them into a community which is to be
faithful to his word and his will. These biblical motifs
of creation, covenant and community provide a foundation for reflection on issues of economic and social
justice.

In the middle of the Exodus story stands the covenant
at Sinai (Ex. 19–24). It begins with an account of
what God has done for the people (Ex. 19:1–6; cf. Jos.
24:1–13) and includes from God's side a promise of
steadfast love *(hesed)* and faithfulness *('emeth,* Ex. 34:-
5–7). The people are summoned to ratify the covenant
by faithfully worshiping God alone and by directing
their lives according to God's *torah,* or sacred teaching, which was made explicit in Israel's great legal
codes such as the Decalogue (Ex. 20:1–17) and the
Book of the Covenant (Ex. 20:22–23:33). Far from
being an arbitrary restriction on the life of the people,
these codes made life in community possible.[4] The
specific laws of the covenant protect human life and

property and demand respect for parents and the spouses and children of one's neighbor. Social interaction is to reflect the norms of the covenant: reciprocal responsibility, mercy and truthfulness. Living like this brings "wholeness" *(shalom)*. The laws manifest a special concern for the vulnerable members of the community: widows, orphans, the poor and strangers in the land. The codes of Israel embody a life freed from slavery: worship of the one God, rejection of idolatry, mutual respect among people, care and protection for every member of the social body. Being free and being a co-responsible community are God's intent for us, according to the Bible.

Just as the experience of the exodus and its covenant provide fundamental experiences of social solidarity which shape subsequent biblical faith, so too the prior life of bondage in Egypt provides a paradigm of oppression (Ex. 1:8–22): labor which benefited only others; the murder of their newborn sons as a way of destroying their future; and the denial of their right to worship the one God (Ex. 5:1–9). In a dramatic reversal, the "bringing forth" from Egypt was the birth of a people truly united with each other as recipients of God's saving gift. Their status before God is intimately connected with the wholeness of the community. Individuals are responsible *before God* both *to* and *for* the community.

After the return from the exile in Babylon (i.e. after 537 B.C.), when Israel combined its traditions into a written *torah* they prefaced to their history as a people the story of the creation of all peoples and of the whole world by the same God who created them as a nation (Gn. 1–11). God is the creator of heaven and earth (Gn. 14:19–22; Is. 40:28; 45:18); creation proclaims his glory (Ps. 89:11) and is very good (Gn. 1:31). Fruitful harvests, bountiful flocks, and a large family are God's blessings on those who heed his word. Such is the joyful refrain that echoes throughout the Bible. One legacy of this theology of creation is the conviction that no dimension of human life lies beyond God's care and concern. God is ever present to creation, and creative engagement with God's handiwork is itself reverence for God.

At the summit of creation stand man and woman, who are in God's image (Gn. 1:26–28). This is the most fundamental affirmation of human dignity. As made in God's image, man and woman are to represent God to the world and to stand before God as partners in dialogue. This dignity comes with human existence prior to any division into races or nations and prior to human labor and human achievement (Gn. 4–11). Men and women are also to share in God's creative activity. They are to be fruitful, to care for the earth (Gn. 2:15) and to have "dominion" over it (Gn. 1:26), but without any suggestion of arbitrary control or selfish use. Rather, creation is a gift; men and women are to be faithful stewards in caring for the earth.[5] They are to continue God's labor in God's image and can "justly consider that by their labor they are unfolding the Creator's work."[6]

To live in the new creation and to be a partner in the new covenant calls us to a sense of community and solidarity as strong as that experienced by the people of the Exodus. Christian baptism unites us not only with the paschal mystery, the death and resurrection of Christ, but through it with all the baptized who through faith are sons and daughters of God (Gal. 3:26–27). This union transcends the divisions of sex, race and social status since "there is neither Jew nor Greek, there is neither slave nor free, there is neither male nor female; for you are all one in Christ Jesus" (Gal. 3:28). The ethical correlative of this common bond makes of the Christian community a place where the strong are to assist the weak (1 Cor. 8:7–13) and rich communities are to come to the aid of poor ones (2 Cor. 8:1–15). Paul expresses the ideal of Christian solidarity succinctly, "Bear one another's burdens and so fulfill the law of Christ" (Gal. 6:2). This solidarity ought to extend not simply to the members of the Christian community, but to all peoples since God wishes all to be saved and to come to the knowledge of the truth (1 Tm. 2:4), and the Christian community is exhorted to do good *to all* (Gal. 6:10).

This vision of creation, covenant and community unfolds within the context of biblical eschatology, the context of our ultimate hope for humanity and for the world. The whole Bible is spanned by the narratives of the first creation (Gn. 1–3) and the vision of a restored creation at the end of history (Rv. 21). Just as creation tells us that God's original design for the world was one of wholeness and unity between God and the human family itself, eschatological imagery offers visions of a restored and renewed creation, a new heaven and a new earth (Is. 66:22). Enmity and hatred will cease (Is. 11:6; 25:1–8), and justice and peace will reign (Is. 26:4–13).

This eschatology, which qualifies all aspects of biblical thought, places human life "between the times," the time of the first and of the restored creation. There will always be a tension between the "already" and the "not yet." Though we live in the new creation, we groan inwardly as we wait for "the redemption of our bodies" (Rom. 8:22–23). In the resurrection of Jesus, death has been conquered, yet we all taste death and await the fullness of the victory over death (1 Cor. 15:51–57). Biblical eschatology means that God's design for human life has been revealed in salvation history, in the exhortations of the prophets, and in the life and teaching of Jesus, but the ultimate realization of God's design is still in the future. Eschatology, however, is not to be identified simply with utopian visions. Christians must embody in their lives the ethos of the new creation while they labor under the weight of the old. Christian eschatology is a counter to a mechanistic pessimism that would remove the course of history from God's hope for history. Christian social ethics will be always a combination of hope and realism. It involves a diagnosis of those sinful structures that continue to alienate the world from God's creative design, as well as the presentation of hopeful alternatives which arise out of the consciousness of living in a renewed creation. Eschatology also cautions against a temptation to see any political or economic system as of ultimate value. The quest for economic and social justice will always take place between prophecy and vision, between realization and hope.

The biblical motifs of creation, covenant and community provide fundamental perspectives and obligatory ideals which should inform our thoughts and our hopes. To stand before God as creator is to respect God's creation, both the world of nature and that of human history. Misuse of the resources of the world or appropriation of them by a minority of the world's population betrays the gift of creation meant for all people who are created in God's image with a mandate to make the earth fruitful. Creation by God and recreation in Christ make us realize that the communality we share with people of other nations is more basic than the barriers national borders create. A true biblical vision of the human condition relativizes the claims of any state or government to total allegiance. It also makes us realize that people of other nations and with other ways of living share equally in God's image and should be equal recipients of God's bounty.

. . .

2. The Primacy of Justice

Characteristic of biblical faith is the insistence that reverence for God as creator and fidelity to the covenant are expressed by an equal reverence and concern for the neighbor. The biblical terms which best summarize this double dimension of biblical faith are *sedaqah,* justice (also translated as righteousness), and *mishpat,* right judgment or justice embodied in a concrete act or deed. The biblical understanding of justice also gives a fundamental perspective to our reflections on social justice and economic issues.[7]

In the Bible Yahweh is described as a "God of justice" (Is. 30:18) who loves justice (Is. 61:8; cf. Pss. 11:7; 33:5; 37:28; 99:4) and delights in it (Jer. 9:24). God executes justice for the needy (Ps. 140:12) and demands justice from the whole people (Dt. 16:20, "Justice and only justice you shall follow that you may live and inherit the land which the Lord your God gives you."). The covenant between God and the people is a betrothal "in righteousness and in justice, in steadfast love and in mercy" (Hos. 2:21). Justice has many levels of meaning. Fundamentally it suggests a sense of what is right or should happen. For example, paths are just when they bring you to your destination, and laws are just when they create harmony within the community. God is "just" by acting as God should, coming to the people's aid when they are in need and summoning them to judgment and conversion when they stray. People are summoned to be "just," that is, to be in a proper relation to God by observing God's laws, which form them into a faithful community. When a society is just, prosperity and blessing result. As Isaiah says, "Justice will bring peace; right will produce calm and security" (32:17, NAB).

A distinctive aspect of the biblical presentation of

justice is that the justice of a community is measured
by its treatment of the powerless in society, most often
described as the widow, the orphan, the poor and the
stranger (non-Israelite) in the land. The major divisions of the Old Testament all show deep concern for
the proper treatment of such people. It is evident in
the laws (Ex. 22:21–27; Dt. 15:1–11), in the Wisdom
tradition (Jb. 29:11–17; Ps. 82:3–4) and the prophetic
literature (esp. Ez. 7:9–10). What these groups of
people have in common is their vulnerability and lack
of power. They are often alone in society and have
no protector or advocate. Therefore it is God who
hears their cries (Pss. 10:14–18; 113:7), and the king
who is God's anointed is commanded to have special
concern for them.

. . . .

When Jesus proclaims, "Seek first the kingdom of
God and his justice" (Mt. 6:33), he is combining two
of the most powerful themes of his biblical heritage.
In understanding and worshiping God as king the
people affirm that God is to be sovereign in their lives
and that they are to live in his realm and manifest his
presence. Jesus preaches a renewed proclamation of
God's kingship and a summons to respond to its demands: "The kingdom of God is at hand; repent and
believe in the Gospel" (Mk. 1:15). To believe in Jesus
is to hear again his summons to conversion.

Like the prophets, Jesus takes the side of those who
are powerless or on the margin of his society such as
the widow (Lk. 7:11–17; Mk. 12:41–44), the Samari-

tan (or stranger in the land, Lk. 17:11–19), the sinful
woman (Lk. 7:36–50) and children (Mk. 10:13–16).
He rejects those religious practices that enable people
to escape the obligation to care for their parents (Mk.
7:9–13) and criticizes the Pharisees because they have
neglected the more important aspects of the law: "justice and mercy and faith" (Mt. 22:23). He tells parables which give hope to the poor and the oppressed
(Lk. 14:7–23; 16:19–31; 18:1–8); and in his description
of the final judgment he says that "all the nations"
will be judged on how they treated him when he was
hungry, thirsty, a stranger, naked, sick and impris-
oned: "As you did it to one of the least of these my
brethren, you did it to me" (Mt. 25:31–46). To turn
aside from those on the margins of society, the needy
and the powerless, is to turn away from Jesus, who
identifies himself with them. Such people present his
face to the world.

3. Wealth and Poverty
Corresponding to the biblical preoccupation with justice for the poor is a pervasive concern with the
dangers of wealth.[8] The goods of the earth are certainly to be enjoyed, and God grants a faithful people
material blessings; but great wealth is seen as a peril.
The rich are wise in their own eyes (Prv. 28:11), are
prone to apostasy and idolatry (Am. 5:4–13; Is. 2:6–8)
as well as to violence and oppression (Am. 4:1–3; Jb.
20:19; Sir. 13:4–7; Jas. 2:6; 5:1–6).
The Gospel of Luke, which was written to a com-

munity that included prosperous Christians, shows
special concern for the dangers of wealth.[9] Jesus pro-
nounces the poor "blessed" and adds a solemn warning, "Woe to you that are rich for you have received
your consolation" (6:19–24). He warns his followers
against covetousness and the notion that life consists
in the abundance of possessions; and he illustrates his
point with the parable of the rich fool whose life is
suddenly snatched away in the midst of his attempts
to secure his wealth (12:13–21), thus illustrating that
"life is more than food and the body more than
clothing" (12:22–23).

In another parable, Jesus depicts the condemnation
of a rich man who does not see the hungry and
suffering Lazarus at his gate. When the rich man
finally "sees" Lazarus, it is from the place of torment
and the opportunity for conversion has passed (16:-
19–31). John Paul II has often recalled this parable to
remind us of our world today where great wealth and
great poverty lie side by side. It is a prophetic warning
to rich nations like the United States to be concerned
for the poorer, less-developed countries.[10] Thus, Luke
presents a synthesis of the biblical concern with
wealth. Wealth is evil when it so dominates a person's
life that it becomes an idol claiming allegiance and
giving security apart from God, or when it blinds a
person to the suffering and needy neighbor. As members of the most prosperous and wealthy nation in the
world, we have special reason to hear the message of
Luke's Gospel addressed to us today.

These biblical perspectives on wealth and poverty form the basis for what today is called "the preferential option for the poor." Shortly before the Second Vatican Council, Pope John XXIII said, "In dealing with the underdeveloped countries, the church presents herself as she is and wants to be—as the church of all people and especially the poor."[11] In *Octogesima Adveniens* Paul VI stated, "In teaching us charity, the Gospel instructs us in the preferential respect due the poor and the special situation they have in society: The more fortunate should renounce some of their rights so as to place their goods more generously at the service of others."[12] Likewise, John Paul II urged the people of our country to have "a special sensitivity toward those who are extremely poor, those suffering from all the physical, mental and moral ills that afflict humanity including hunger, neglect, unemployment and despair."[13]

It was at the meeting of the Latin American bishops in Puebla, Mexico, that the term "option for the poor" emerged as a significant category in church thinking.[14] In his addresses in Brazil in the following year, John Paul II described the option for the poor as "a call to have a special openness with the small and the weak, those that suffer and weep, those that are humiliated and left on the margin of society, so as to help them win their dignity as human persons and children of God."[15] He then noted that this option is not just for Christians, but for everyone in society who is "concerned with the true common good."[16]

. . .

Throughout the Gospels Jesus comes to people engaged in the ordinary activities of life and summons them to follow him (Mk. 2:14–15). Saying yes involves not just the leaving of family and friends, but a positive attachment to Jesus, "imitating the pattern of his life, not just walking after him."[17] The "pattern" of Jesus' life was to be obedient to God's will and to respond to God's presence in his life and teaching. He confronted the power of evil (Mk. 1:21–28), healed the sick (Mk. 1:29–34), fed the hungry (Mk. 6:30–44) and attacked hardness of heart (Mk. 3:5; 8:17). In his parables Jesus took the everyday world of his hearers, the world of farming and fishing, of buying and selling, of weddings and feasts, and showed them that it is in this world that they meet God and find salvation.

. . .

Our sense of community is also fostered by the memories we share as descendants of immigrants who came often as aliens to a strange land. The stories of our past remind us of the times when our church was a defender of the defenseless and a voice for the voiceless. Today, as many Catholics achieve greater economic prosperity, we are tempted like the people of the Exodus to forget the powerless and the stranger in our midst. The church must hear them and speak for them. Also, as John Paul II has most recently reminded us, the church, like the Samaritan of Luke's Gospel (10:29–37), must acquire a "sensitivity of heart which bears witness to compassion toward a suffering person."[18] Like the Samaritan, we too are called to "stop" and enter into the world of the neighbor with effective and liberating care.

. . .

B. Living as Disciples Today: From the Bible to Economic Ethics

This summary of the biblical vision of economic life presents all Christians in the United States with a great challenge, both as individuals and as members of society. The renewal of the church's understanding of the biblical message in recent decades has done a great deal to deepen awareness of the Christian vocation to pursue greater justice in social and economic life. The Catholic tradition, however, has long recognized that the Bible, taken alone, does not provide direct solutions to complex policy questions. Our reflections on U.S. economic life must be informed by the biblical vision of kingdom and discipleship, but they must also attend carefully to the long postbiblical tradition of the church, to philosophical analysis of basic social norms, and to the experience and urgent problems of contemporary men and women. These other resources for moral analysis of U.S. economic life are important for several reasons.

. . .

Catholic social teaching seeks to contribute to the public debate on economic policy. In addressing policy questions in a pluralistic society, the church does not presume that everyone shares its religious vision or that its theological arguments will be persuasive to all members of the body politic. Therefore Catholic teaching seeks to support its perspectives on policy with arguments based on philosophical reasoning and empirical analysis. We hope that such arguments will be persuasive not only to Catholics but also to other Christians, Jews and citizens at large. The importance of this philosophical and empirical reasoning takes added force from the Catholic conviction that human understanding and religious belief are complementary, not contradictory. In this letter we rely on both faith and reason, and we hope to show their mutual interdependence.

. . .

Men and women cannot grow to full self-realization in isolation. This realization takes place in interaction, interdependence, communication, collaboration, and —in the fullest form—communion and love. Such fullness of community is a goal which we long for and will finally achieve when God's reconciling work in Christ comes to completion in the kingdom. Reflection on experience shows vividly that any genuine respect for human dignity demands that we cultivate and strengthen the bonds of solidarity among us.

. . .

This Christian and human vision grounds our conviction that communal solidarity and mutual responsibility must characterize an economy that truly respects persons. The development of social, economic and political means to exercise mutual responsibility is one of the most urgent challenges facing the U.S. and global economies today. All we say in this letter about the ethical principles of economic life flows from this conviction and represents an attempt to show its implications for personal behavior and public policy. Concurring with the teachings of the Second Vatican Council and recent popes, we are convinced that an emphasis on solidarity and interdependence will enable the evangelical message of Jesus Christ to help renew the economic life of our nation and our world.

II. ETHICAL NORMS FOR ECONOMIC LIFE

. . .

A. Human Rights: The Minimum Conditions for Life in Community

Modern Catholic social teaching has made its moral perspective specific in a detailed exposition of the fundamental duties and basic human rights of all persons. The church's understanding of these duties and rights has undergone considerable development. In recent centuries the church has learned much from the larger society in which it exists about specific conditions for the social protection of human dignity.[1] Especially in recent years it has sought to contribute to the building of a more human society by advocating enhanced respect for the rights of all.

. . .

All economic activity, when it is rightly ordered, has a threefold moral significance. First, it embodies the distinctive human capacity for self-realization and self-expression. Neither money, machines nor animals work in this sense. Only persons do. Thus economic activity should be an expression of the distinctive dignity of human persons, who have been created in the image of God.[2] Second, work is one of the chief ways that human beings seek self-fulfillment, both the fulfillment of their basic material needs and the spiritual need to express initiative and creativity. Finally, work should enable everyone to make a contribution to the human community to the extent each is able. Work is not only for oneself. It is also for one's family and for others. Every working person's activity in the economy should be a productive contribution to the common good of the nation while also serving "to add to the heritage of the whole human family, of all the people living in the world."[3]

Therefore, if the economy is to function in a way that respects the dignity of persons, these qualities should be present: *It should enable persons to find a significant measure of self-realization in their labor; it should permit persons to fulfill their material needs through adequate remuneration; and it should make possible the enhancement of unity and solidarity within the family, the nation and the world community.*

It is within this broad framework that Catholic social teaching has developed its understanding of the basic rights and duties of persons in the economic sphere. Everyone has a legitimate claim on economic benefits to at least the minimum level necessary for the social protection of human dignity. No one can be legitimately excluded or abandoned by the larger community in its activity. The economic minimum owed to every person by society is made explicit in the human-rights standards affirmed in church teaching. These rights have been most systematically outlined by Pope John XXIII in his encyclical "Peace on Earth." It will be useful to recall them here.

In the first place stand the rights to "food, clothing, shelter, rest, medical care." These express the absolute minimum for the protection of human life. In order to ensure their protection, certain social guarantees are indispensable. These include "the right to security in case of sickness, inability to work, widowhood, old age, unemployment, or in any other case in which one is deprived of the means of subsistence through no fault of one's own." Further, all persons have rights "to free initiative in the economic field and the right to work." They have the right to "working conditions in which physical health is not endangered," to "carry on economic activities according to the degree of responsibility of which one is capable" and to wages sufficient to guarantee one's family "a standard of living in keeping with human dignity."[4]

. . .

Both the Christian faith and the common experience we share as human beings should convince us that these basic economic rights demand respect if our economic life is to be worthy of our humanity. Though these economic rights are not listed in our Bill of Rights, their spirit was familiar to many of our ancestors. For example, the first Pilgrims on the shores of New England pledged themselves to be a community bound together by just such mutual respect: "For this end, we must be knit together in this work as one man, we must entertain each other in brotherly affection, we must be willing to abridge ourselves of our superfluities, for the supply of others' necessities."[5] The fulfillment of this pledge is the foundation of any truly humane economic order. Both as individuals and as a nation, it is the standard by which we will be judged by God and the opinion of humankind.

When we consider the performance of the American economy and its success in respecting these basic economic rights, we see an encouraging record. In its comparatively short history the United States has made impressive strides in the effort to provide material necessities, employment, health care, education and social services for its people. It has done this within a political system based on the precious value of freedom. While the United States can be rightfully proud of its achievements as a society, we know full well that there have been failures, some of them massive and ugly. Hunger persists in our country, as our church-sponsored soup kitchens testify. Far too many people are homeless and must seek refuge from the cold in our church basements. As pastors we know the despair that can devastate individuals, families and whole communities when the plague of unemployment strikes. Inadequate funding for education puts a high mortgage on our economic future. Racial discrimination has devastating effects on the economic well-being of minorities. Inequality in employment opportunity, low wages for women and lack of sufficient child-care services can undermine family life. The blighted and decaying environment of some disadvantaged communities stands in stark contrast with the natural and architectural beauty of others. Real space for leisure, contemplation and prayer seems increasingly scarce in our driven society.

. . .

Overcoming these obstacles will be an onerous task. It must begin with the formation of a new cultural consensus that *all persons really do have rights in the economic sphere* and that society has a moral obligation to take the necessary steps to ensure that no one among us is hungry, homeless, unemployed or otherwise denied what is necessary to live with dignity.

. . .

This economic challenge we all face today has many parallels with the political challenge that confronted the founders of our nation. In order to create a new kind of political democracy they were compelled to develop ways of thinking and political institutions which had never existed before. Their efforts were arduous and imperfectly realized, but they launched an experiment in the protection of civil and political rights that has prospered through the efforts of those who came after them. We believe the time has come for a similar experiment in economic democracy: the creation of an order that guarantees the minimum conditions of human dignity in the economic sphere for every person. By drawing on the resources of the Catholic moral-religious tradition, we hope to make a contribution to such a new "American experiment" in this letter.

B. Justice, Power and Institutional Priorities

This struggle for the economic rights of all will not succeed if we slacken our efforts of thought and will when faced with hard choices. We must establish reasonable priorities that make these rights genuine policy objectives rather than mere pious wishes. The church's tradition has developed and refined fundamental norms of justice drawn from the Gospel and human reason which can guide our efforts.

In Catholic social teaching, the notion of justice is a rich concept with a number of different dimensions. Without exhaustively analyzing this entire complex of ideas, it will be useful to take note of some key aspects of it which can help us establish priorities for U.S. economic institutions today.

In line with our insistence on the indispensability of human dignity and social solidarity it is clear that *justice demands the establishment of minimum levels of participation by all persons in the life of the human community.* The ultimate injustice is for a person or group to be actively treated or passively abandoned as a non-member of the moral community which is the human race. This can take many forms. Murder is the most atrocious and obvious example. Recent Catholic teaching has spoken of many other forms which result from the patterns of institutional organization and distribution of power in contemporary society. These can all be described as forms of "marginalization."[6]

Marginalization can take a political shape, as when a person or group is denied access to influence on public decision making through denial of free speech, through outright repression by the state or through an inordinate concentration of political power in the hands of a few. Marginalization can also take economic forms which can be equally destructive of human dignity and community. Within the United States individuals, families and local communities can fall victim to a downward cycle of poverty generated by economic forces that they are increasingly powerless to influence the poorer they become. For example, men and women are thrown out of work as a result of plant closings or national policies they are too weak to change precisely because they are unemployed or unorganized. Farm families today are frequently driven off the land because their small farms cannot compete with large agribusinesses that have easy access to credit and large government subsidies. Elderly people become homeless because they lack the resources to purchase the apartment they live in when the owner converts the building into a condominium in a neighborhood undergoing gentrification. This pattern is even more severe beyond our borders in the least developed countries. Whole nations are prevented from participating in the international economic order because they lack both the resources to do so and the power to change their disadvantaged position. Moreover, persons living in absolute poverty in the less-developed countries are excluded from sharing in even the meager resources available in their homelands. In short, marginalized persons are those who have "no voice and no choice."[7]

·   ·   ·

In relating the notion of justice-as-participation to economic life in the United States today, several more specific points are important. *First, justice is not simply a matter of seeing to it that people's private needs are fulfilled. It is also a matter of enabling them to be active and productive.* Human needs will be fulfilled in a human way when persons are enabled to share actively in the economic life of the community. The notion of "social justice," which has a technical meaning in Catholic moral theology, stresses the obligation and right of all to make productive contributions to the life of society as a whole. In the words of Pius XI, "It is of the very essence of social justice to demand from each individual all that is necessary for the common good."[8] The notion of social justice thus includes an obligation to create the goods, services and invested wealth that are necessary for social well-being.

·   ·   ·

We believe that the level of inequality in income and wealth in our society and even more the inequality on the world scale today must be judged morally unacceptable according to these criteria. Our discussions and study during the preparation of this letter lead us to the same conclusion reached by the 1971 Synod of Bishops: "Unless combated by social and political action, the influence of the new industrial and technological order favors the concentration of wealth, power and decision making in the hands of a small public or private controlling group."[9] This concentration of economic privilege derives in large part from institutional relationships which enable certain persons and groups to participate more actively and powerfully in economic life. Disparity of talent or of desire to work does not sufficiently explain this situation. These institutional patterns and power relationships must be examined and revised if we are to achieve greater justice in society. In Part 2 of this letter we shall outline certain changes we believe justice calls for both domestically and internationally.

Unequal distribution of income, education, wealth, job opportunities or other economic goods on the basis of race, sex or any other arbitrary standard, can never be justified. As the Second Vatican Council forcefully stated: "With respect to the fundamental rights of the person, every type of discrimination, whether social or cultural, whether based on sex, race, color, social condition, language or religion, is to be overcome and eradicated as contrary to God's in-

tent."[10] The elimination of such patterns of discrimination throughout economic and social life is an urgent moral duty for our society. Persons who make
comparable contributions to society are entitled to
comparable rewards. Further, the most fundamental
obligation of justice is that no person be excluded
from a reasonable level of participation in the full life
of society. Where this right has been denied by past
discrimination and the continuing effects of this discrimination persist today, society has the obligation to
take positive steps to overcome the legacy of injustice.
We believe that judiciously administered affirmative
actions programs in education and employment can be
important expressions of that drive for solidarity and
participation which is at the heart of true justice. This
conclusion simply applies the general principle that
persons with special needs deserve special treatment if
their equal dignity is to be respected. It is a principle
which is especially applicable when these needs have
been caused by society's unjust actions in the past.
Social harm calls for social relief.

We can summarize the implications of these norms
of justice in several priority principles which should
shape our economic policies and institutions both domestically and internationally.

*The fulfillment of the basic needs of the poor is of the
highest priority.* Personal decisions, social policies and
power relationships must all be evaluated by their
effects on those who lack the minimum necessities of
nutrition, housing, education and health care. Our

society has to consider other goals than these, such as productivity and economic efficiency, but not to the further detriment of the disadvantaged of our world. This evaluation of decisions, policies and institutions primarily in light of their impact on the poor constitutes the "preferential option for the poor" which flows from biblical faith. It is also a priority fully supported by human experience and reason. In particular, this principle grants priority to meeting fundamental human needs over the fulfillment of desires for luxury consumer goods or for profits that do not ultimately benefit the common good of the community.

Increased economic participation for the marginalized takes priority over the preservation of privileged concentrations of power, wealth and income. This principle follows from the fact that economic rights and responsibilities must find expression in the institutional order of society. It grants priority to policies and programs that enhance participation through work. It also points out the need for policies to improve the situation of groups unjustly discriminated against in the past. And it has very important implications for the institutions that shape the international economic order.

Meeting human needs and increasing participation should be priority targets in the investment of wealth, talent and human energy. Increasing productivity both in the United States and in less-developed parts of the world is a clear need. But different sorts of investment of human and financial resources can have very different outcomes for people even when they have similar rates of productivity. This principle presents a strong moral challenge to policies that put large amounts of talent and capital into the production of luxury consumer goods and military technology while failing to invest sufficiently in education, in the basic infrastructure of our society or in economic sectors that produce the jobs, goods and services that we urgently need.

These three priorities are not policies. Rather they are norms which should guide the economic choices of all the diverse actors in our society and help shape economic institutions. They are norms which can help the United States move closer to the goal of protecting the basic economic rights of all persons. They were strongly affirmed as implications of Catholic social teaching by Pope John Paul II during his recent trip to Canada: "The needs of the poor take priority over the desires of the rich; the rights of workers over the maximization of profits; the preservation of the environment over uncontrolled industrial expansion; production to meet social needs over production for military purposes."[11] There will undoubtedly be disputes about the concrete implications of these priorities in our complex world. We do not seek to foreclose discussion about these implications. We do believe, however, that a serious effort by our country to move in the direction they indicate will be of great benefit both to the people of the United States and of the nations linked with us in a global economy.

*C. The Responsibilities and Rights of Diverse
Economic Agents and Institutions*

These principles present the U.S. economy with a powerful moral challenge. They call our country to build on its past achievements and to direct its economy onto paths which will better serve both the national and international common good. But simply proclaiming that poverty should be eliminated, unemployment abolished, discrimination ended, and education and leisure made available to all is not enough. We must also reflect more concretely on who is actually responsible for bringing about the necessary changes.

. . .

To this end, we now want to indicate how various kinds of economic actors, both individual and institutional, can foster greater economic justice. These include: working people and labor unions; managers, investors, business enterprises and banks; citizens and governments; transnational enterprises and international economic agencies; consumers; and finally the church itself.

1. Working People and Labor Unions

. . .

Because work is so important in contributing to personal, familial and social well-being, people have a right to work. In addition, in return for their labor, workers have a right to a just wage. Labor is not simply a commodity traded on the open market nor is a just wage determined simply by the level the market will sustain. As Pope Leo XIII stated, every working person "has the right of securing things to sustain life."[12] It is one of the consequences of the way power is distributed in a free-market economy that employers frequently possess greater bargaining power than do employees in the negotiation of wage agreements. Such unequal power may press workers into a choice between an inadequate wage and no wage at all. The provision of a wage sufficient to support a family in dignity is necessary to prevent this exploitation of workers. The dignity of workers also requires adequate health care, insurance for old age or disability, healthful working conditions, weekly rest and periodic holidays for recreation and leisure.[13] These provisions are all essential if workers are to be treated as persons rather than simply as a "factor of production." Justice, not charity, demands such minimum guarantees.

As an institutional means to achieve these guarantees the church fully supports the right of workers to form unions or other associations to secure their rights to fair wages and working conditions. This is a specific application of the more general right to associate. Trade unions express the essentially social nature of human persons and manifest the human need for solidarity. In the words of Pope John Paul II, "The experience of history teaches that organizations of this type are an indispensable element of social life, especially in modern industrialized societies."[14] Unions may also legitimately resort to strikes in situations where they are the only available means for pursuing the justice owed to workers.[15] No one may deny the right to organize for purposes of collective bargaining or coercively suppress unions without attacking human dignity itself. Therefore we firmly oppose organized efforts, such as those regrettably now seen in this country, to break existing unions or to prevent workers from organizing through intimidation and threats. U.S. labor-law reform is needed to give greater substance to the right to organize, to prevent intimidation of workers and to provide remedies in a more timely manner for unfair labor practices.

This sort of threat to human dignity has been pursued ruthlessly in many countries beyond our borders —both by those built on socialist principles and by those who espouse capitalist economics. We vehemently oppose such violations of the freedom to associate wherever they occur, for they represent an intolerable attack on social solidarity.

Along with these rights of workers and unions go a number of important responsibilities. Individual workers have obligations to their employers, and trade unions also have duties to society as a whole. They must not use their collective power to press demands whose fulfillment would damage the rights of others. Racial and sexual discrimination has sometimes marred the exercise of power by U.S. trade unions. Organized labor has an important responsibility to work positively toward eliminating the effects of the injustice this discrimination has caused. Trade unions must not press for ever-higher wage levels for their members when the predictable outcome will be rising unemployment, especially for the unorganized sector of the labor market. As Pope John Paul II has observed:

"Just efforts to secure the rights of workers who are united by the same profession should always take into account the limitations imposed by the general economic situation of the country. Union demands cannot be turned into a kind of group or class 'egoism.' "[16]

. . .

2. Managers, Investors, Businesses and Banks

The ability of the U.S. economy to fulfill the demands of justice depends both on the way the country uses its great wealth and on the responsible management of its economic resources. Persons who own property, who invest their financial resources and who manage enterprises that determine the economic health of the country can all make most important contributions to a more just society. As Pope John Paul II has pointed out, "The degree of well-being which society enjoys today would be unthinkable without the dynamic figure of the businessperson, whose function consists of organizing human labor and the means of production so as to give rise to the goods and services necessary for the prosperity and progress of the community."[17] The rights and responsibilities of persons engaged in business and finance flow from the dual necessity of both protecting their freedom to make these contributions and ensuring that this freedom is accountable to the norms of justice and the common good of society.

. . .

The responsibilities of the business and financial sectors are expressions of the duty to exercise faithful stewardship over the resources with which God has blessed our society. We have great wealth, both in fertile land and natural resources. In addition, the ingenuity and inventiveness of our forebears have left us a legacy of vast industrial and technological capacity. Those in our society who own and manage this wealth hold it in trust, both for all who depend on it today as well as for generations yet to come. As St. Paul observed, "What is expected of stewards is that each one be found worthy of his trust" (1 Cor. 4:2).

This concept of stewardship should be reflected in the policies and institutional structures of businesses and financial institutions. In using economic resources the fundamental principle should be that, whatever one's legal entitlement, no one can ever own these resources absolutely or use them without regard for others. As Psalm 24 proclaims, "The earth is the Lord's and the fullness thereof." God is the only real owner; human beings are the trustees of the goods given them.

This applies first of all to the land and other natural resources. Their use must be governed by the need to preserve the fertility of farmland and the integrity of the environment. Short-term profits reaped at the cost of topsoil erosion or toxic contamination violate this trust. The resources created by human industry and ingenuity are also held in trust. As Pope John Paul II has stated: "This gigantic and powerful instrument— the whole collection of the means of production that in a sense are considered synonymous with 'capital'— is the result of work and bears the signs of human labor."[18]

Within the framework of this basic vision of steward-ship and concern for the common good, the Catholic tradition has long defended the right to private own-ership of property.[19] Private ownership has value for many reasons. It provides incentives for diligence at work. It allows parents to contribute to the welfare of their children. Directly and indirectly it protects political liberty. In the words of John XXIII, "experi-ence and history testify that where political regimes do not allow to private individuals the possession also of productive goods, the exercise of human liberty is violated or completely destroyed in matters of pri-mary importance."[20] The protection of this right is therefore a significant prerequisite of a just economic policy. It opens up space in society for the exercise of forms of creativity and initiative which can genuinely serve both individuals and the common good. For these reasons ownership should be a possibility for as broad a part of our population as possible.[21] Small and medium-sized farms, small businesses and innovative entrepreneurial enterprises of moderate scale are among the more creative and efficient sectors of our economy. Pope John XXIII encouraged the body politic "to modify economic and social life so that the way is made easier for widespread private possession of such things as durable goods, homes, gardens, tools requisite for artisan enterprises and family-type farms, investments in enterprises of medium and large size."[22] We believe this recommendation remains a valid one for the United States today.

This support of private ownership does not mean that any individual, group, organization or nation has the right to unlimited accumulation of wealth. Especially when there are so many needy people in our world, the right to own must bow to the higher principles of stewardship and the common use of the goods of creation. There is a "social mortgage" on private property[23] which implies that "private property does not constitute for anyone an absolute or unconditioned right. No one is justified in keeping for his exclusive use what he does not need, when others lack necessities."[24] In our increasingly complex economy, true stewardship may also sometimes demand that the right to own cede to public involvement in the planning or ownership of certain sectors of the economy. The church's teaching opposes collectivist and statist economic approaches. But it also resists the notion that an unimpeded market automatically produces justice. Therefore, as Pope John Paul II has argued, "one cannot exclude the socialization, in suitable conditions, of certain means of production."[25] The determination of when such conditions exist must

be made on a case-by-case basis in light of the demands of the common good.

To carry out these responsibilities and secure these
rights in the business and financial sectors will require
a lively sense of moral responsibility on the part of
individuals as well as a prudent adjustment of social
accountability. The work of business people, managers, investors and financiers is a genuine Christian
vocation when carried out as a form of stewardship.
We wish to encourage and support a needed renewal
of this sense of vocation in the business community.
We also recognize that the way business serves the
good of society depends very much on the incentives
created by tax policy, the availability of credit and
other forms of public policy at various governmental
levels. These should be shaped in a way that encourages the goals outlined here.

3. Citizens and Government

In addition to the moral claims related to one's specific
place on the institutional map of the economy, all
people have obligations based simply on their membership in the social community itself. In the fulfillment of these duties a society becomes a true
commonwealth. All have obligations toward the poor
and are duty-bound to come to their assistance. Indeed, the Christian tradition regards the treatment of
the poor as the litmus test of the justice or injustice
of a community. Voluntary donation of money, time
and talent to those in need is a Christian imperative

arising from God's command that we love our neighbor as ourselves. It is also an expression of the fundamental human solidarity which binds us together in a moral community. Voluntary action to overcome the wounds of injustice through almsgiving, sharing possessions, hospitality and other forms of charitable assistance is part of the Christian vocation and the duty of all human beings.

Such acts of charity are, at their best, attempts to heal the pain which injustice causes. But all have a larger responsibility to remove the causes of this injustice in the community. This is our responsibility as citizens—a personal responsibility to be exercised through government and the political process. Catholic social thought has long held that one of government's prime tasks is the coordination and regulation of the activities of diverse groups in society in a way that leads to the common good and the protection of basic rights. In the words of Pope Paul VI, "As social beings persons build up their destiny within a series of groupings which demand, as their completion and as the necessary condition for their development, a vaster society, one of universal character, the political society."[26] The obligations of justice in the economic sphere, therefore, have a political component which falls on individual citizens acting through their government in a democratic society.

In particular, government has the responsibility to guarantee the provision and maintenance of the economy's infrastructure: such things as roads, bridges, harbors, and means of public communication and transport. It should regulate trade and commerce in the interest of fairness. It has a specific obligation to assist the poor, the disadvantaged, the handicapped, the unemployed and others who lack the means to care for themselves. It should assume a positive role in the generation of employment and the establishment of fair labor practices.[27] Government may levy the taxes necessary to meet these responsibilities, and citizens have a moral obligation to pay those taxes.

. . .

Government, therefore, has a moral function: that of enabling citizens to coordinate their actions to protect basic rights and ensure economic justice for all members of the commonwealth.

While affirming the positive role of government, Catholic social thought does not advocate a statist approach to economic policy. It resists excessive concentration of power in the hands of government, for this can itself threaten human rights and justice. The primary norm for determining the scope and limits of governmental intervention is the "principle of subsidiarity" enunciated by Pius XI and reaffirmed by later popes. This principle states that government should undertake only those initiatives necessary for protecting basic justice which exceed the capacity of individuals or private groups acting independently. In Pius XI's words, the principle states that the government "should furnish help *(subsidium)* to the members of the social body and never destroy or absorb them."[28]

. . .

The following are some of the areas we believe need
the particular attention of various levels of government today. Overcoming unemployment demands
as a prerequisite the provision of appropriate education and training and more adequate financing.
Meeting the material needs of the poor requires the
restructuring of the delivery of social services.
Eliminating current patterns of discrimination and
the effects of past discrimination also requires governmental action. Similarly, in the international
sphere, government must look to the effects of our
economic choices on other nations, especially the
less-developed countries. We shall discuss these questions at greater length below. Though government
cannot solve these problems by itself, they cannot be
addressed adequately without governmental involvement on a variety of local and national levels. We
urgently need a new political will to pursue these
objectives as a society.

4. Transnational and International Economic
   Actors

Since World War II one of the most important patterns of change in economic life has been its growing
internationalization. We can neither understand the
problems of the U.S. economy today nor propose
plausible solutions to these problems without giving
the most serious attention to the links that bind us to
the rest of the world.

. . .

The situation of global interdependence is a fact. It is evident in the way U.S. jobs are increasingly vulnerable to competition from industries in other nations, both developed and developing. U.S. financial institutions would surely face serious crises should Third-World nations be forced to default on their huge debts. The less-developed countries of the world, with vast numbers of people living in absolute poverty within their borders, depend heavily on the trade, monetary, financial and aid policies of the developed countries.

. . . . .

Unless consciously directed in ways that seek to protect human dignity and build greater solidarity across borders, interdependence can be a source of increased conflict and danger. This danger threatens both our own relatively strong economy and even more so the fragile economies of developing nations. Thus we have an urgent duty to direct our attention to what Pope John Paul II referred to as "the quality of interdependence in our global economy."[29]

The conviction that the human race is one moral community must be the basis for the effort to improve the quality of global interdependence. As bishops our response to this challenge derives from a theological truth: "the unity of the human family—rooted in common creation, destined for the kingdom, and united by moral bonds of rights and duties."[30] We recognize the legitimate function of the nation-state as an instrument of justice in a world made up of diverse cultures, with different traditions and various ways of structuring their economies. But national boundaries cannot attain an absolute moral significance in either the political or economic domain. This is neither economically possible nor morally acceptable.

5. Consumers

We measure the justice of our economic institutions in part by their ability to deliver those goods and services which fulfill basic human needs and provide a living worthy of human dignity. In our economy consumption is a stimulus to production, and increased production generates employment. As consumers, therefore, all of us play an important role in the pursuit of economic justice.

Nevertheless, both our Christian faith and the norms of human justice impose distinct limits on what we consume and how we view material goods. The Gospel calls us to renounce disordered attachment to earthly possessions. Jesus blessed the poor, though he did not teach that degrading poverty is somehow a blessed condition. He called us to seek first the kingdom of God rather than an ever-increasing store of goods and wealth. Similarly, the earliest Christians sought to alleviate poverty and called upon the wealthy in their community to relinquish their goods in the service of their brothers and sisters. Such limits on consumption and the accumulation of wealth are essential if we are to avoid what Pope Paul VI called "the most evident form of moral underdevelopment," namely avarice.[31] They are also essential to the realization of the justice that protects human dignity.

. . .

A second concern is the tendency to consume rather than save available resources. If we as a nation want to protect the rights of the poor more effectively, we must save and invest in both the private and public sectors of our economy. Saving accumulates personal resources for the future, but it also represents an investment in the productive capacity of the nation to provide needed work and a decent livelihood for all. Conversely, excessive consumption threatens the well-being of future generations and violates the obligations of stewardship. Provided that savings and investments are shaped by the priorities outlined above, they can make a significant contribution to our ability to live up to the demands of justice. A consumerist mentality which encourages immediate gratification mortgages our future and ultimately risks undermining the foundations of a just order. Both our cultural values and our tax structures need to be revised to discourage excessively high levels of consumption and to encourage saving and consequent investment in both private and public endeavors that promote the economic rights of all persons.

6. The Church

We have undertaken the task of writing this letter as an exercise of the teaching ministry which is ours as bishops. We would be negligent in our duties, however, were we to overlook the fact that the church is not only a teacher, but is itself an actor in the economic domain. The church employs large numbers of people in its parishes, schools, hospitals and social agencies. It also has relatively modest investments for the support of its work. As bishops we are responsible for the stewardship and effective management of the resources which many generous people have given the community of the church to enable it to carry out the mission of Christ. All the moral principles that govern the just operation of any economic endeavor apply to the church and its many agencies and institutions.

Indeed the church should be exemplary in its fidelity to the principles of economic justice and its commitment to the protection of the rights of all who are associated with it. As the 1971 Synod of Bishops in Rome reminded us:

"While the church is bound to give witness to justice, she recognizes that anyone who ventures to speak to people about justice must first be just in their eyes. Hence we must undertake an examination of the modes of acting and of the possessions and lifestyle found within the church herself."[32]

. . .

The effective implementation of these objectives will strain the church's resources. This is the plight we as bishops share with many others who hold the responsibilities we do as administrators. We pledge that we will seek in every way possible to reduce other expenses in order to improve our ability to provide adequate wages and benefits.

. . . .

All church institutions must also fully recognize the rights of employees to organize and bargain collectively with the institution through whatever association or organization they freely choose without undue pressures from their employers or from already existing labor organizations.[33]

. . . .

Individual Christians and church-related institutions that are shareholders in U.S. corporations must also make efforts to ensure that the invested funds are used responsibly. Pursuit of an adequate return on investment for the support of the work of the church is a moral and legal fiduciary responsibility of the trustees of church-related institutions. It is not, however, their sole responsibility. As part owners they can help shape the policies of these companies by dialogue with management, by the way they exercise their right to vote at annual corporate meetings through proxies, by introducing resolutions for the consideration of other shareholders and by their decisions about investment or divestment. The questions faced by shareholders in exercising these responsibilities are often complex, so we urge that they be approached with the necessary care. We believe this is an area where the church can be both a teacher and an agent of economic justice.

The church has a special call to be a servant of the

poor, the sick and the marginalized of our world. We have many professional persons and volunteers in our community who work hard and long to carry out this task. But more needs to be done. We do not accept the view that private agencies such as the church are the primary agents of care for those who are hurting in our country. All citizens bear this responsibility, and it should be carried out through their government as we have argued above. But we do know that the church cannot close its heart or its doors to the victims of injustice when our society fails to live up to its duties. This applies not only to clergy, religious and others who work full time in the church. Lay men and women in a wide array of vocations have great opportunities to carry out this mission which belongs to every member of the Christian community. We know many of them—teachers, homemakers, laborers, lawyers, politicians and numerous others—who have used their skills and their compassion to seek innovative ways to carry out the goals we are proposing in this letter. As they do this they *are* the church, acting for economic justice. Grass-roots efforts by the poor themselves are also indispensable. The Christian community can learn much from the way our deprived brothers and sisters assist each other in their struggle. We both invite and challenge more of our number in the Christian community to hear the words of Jesus, first spoken when he exhorted his hearers to imitate the Samaritan who saw a fellow human in need, had compassion on him and interrupted his

journey to come to his aid: "Go and do likewise" (Lk.
10:37).

PART TWO

POLICY APPLICATIONS

The principles of Catholic social teaching provide a
rich tradition from which to approach a discussion of
economic justice. They form the basis for the reflections on specific public-policy issues that will be addressed in this section. We shall attempt here to focus
the light of moral principles on certain of the economic realities and choices that are central to American life. In doing so, we are aware that the movement
from principle to practice is a complex and sometimes
difficult task. We undertake this task with the firm
conviction that moral values have an important role
to play in determining public policies, but with the
understanding that ethical principles in themselves do
not dictate specific kinds of programs or provide blue-
prints for action. Rather, our principles must interact
with empirical data, with historical, social and political realities, and with competing demands for limited
resources. The effectiveness of our prudential judgments in this area will depend not only on the moral
force of our principles, but also on the empirical
accuracy of our information and our assumptions.

The specific topics we have chosen to address here
are the following: 1) employment; 2) poverty; 3) food

and agriculture; 4) collaborating to shape economic policy; and 5) international economic concerns. This is not intended to be a comprehensive analysis of the U.S. economy. Numerous important issues which one could legitimately expect to be here will not be treated in the document. Other issues are touched on only briefly. We emphasize, therefore, that these are illustrative topics intended to exemplify the interaction of moral values and economic issues in our day, not to encompass all such values and issues. This document is not a technical blueprint for economic reform, but rather an attempt to foster a serious moral analysis of economic justice.

. . .

We recognize that in certain cases the same principles interpreted differently or combined with other assumptions may lead to different conclusions. We affirm in this context what we said in the pastoral letter "The Challenge of Peace":

"We do not intend that our treatment of each of these issues carry the same moral authority as our statement of universal moral principles and formal church teaching. Indeed, we stress here at the beginning that not every statement in this letter has the same moral authority. At times we reassert universally binding moral principles. At still other times we reaffirm statements of recent popes and the teaching of Vatican II. Again, at other times we apply moral principles to specific cases.

"When making applications of these principles we

realize—and we wish readers to recognize—that prudential judgments are involved based on specific circumstances which can change or which can be
interpreted differently by people of good will. However, the moral judgments that we make in specific
cases, while not binding in conscience, are to be given
serious attention and consideration by Catholics as
they determine whether their moral judgments are
consistent with the Gospel" (No. 9–10).

We expect that on complex economic questions a
diversity of opinions on specific policy applications
will exist, even among those who hold the same moral
principles. We believe that such differences on policy
issues should be expressed within the framework of
Catholic moral teaching, and we urge mutual respect
among different groups as they carry on this dialogue.
For this process of reflection and dialogue will be
most constructive if it is characterized not only by
conviction and commitment, but also by civility and
charity.

Although we address in this letter only a limited
number of economic issues, we believe that it is both
desirable and necessary to have serious moral reflection and dialogue on the full range of topics that are
part of the quest for economic justice; and we encourage others to carry on this task. Such explicit reflection on the ethical content of economic choices and
policies must become an integral part of the way in
which we relate our religious belief to the realities of
everyday life.

III. EMPLOYMENT

The most urgent priority for U.S. domestic economic policy is the creation of new jobs with adequate pay and decent working conditions. The prime goal must be to make it possible for everyone who is seeking a job to find employment which befits human dignity. As we noted above, Pope John Paul II has written that human work is a key to the whole social question.

There are many forms of work which express human dignity and contribute to society, not all of them in the formal job market. Homemakers, students, artists and those whose lives are devoted to enhancing the spiritual life of the community deserve respect and support. Nevertheless a job with adequate pay should be available to all who seek one. This right protects the freedom and obligation of all to participate in the economic life of society and flows from the priorities of justice we have outlined above. Employment is crucial to self-realization for the worker and to the fulfillment of material needs. It also forms the first line of defense against poverty. Work with adequate pay rather than welfare should be available to all who are able and willing to undertake it. Persons working full time should receive wages and other social benefits adequate to ensure that they and their families do not fall into poverty. Income for families should also be sufficient to enable one of the parents to spend time at home devoted to the care and education of small children, without prejudice to the equal rights of men and women in family and society.[1] To meet these basic demands of human dignity will require an increased number of good jobs. Job creation will benefit society as well as the worker, for it will enable more persons to contribute to the common good and to the productivity required to meet human needs.

Though the task of securing jobs for all who seek them is both enormous and complex, we believe that it can be done. The ability of a dynamic U.S. economy to generate millions of new jobs in the past several decades provides precedent for the belief that the goal is achievable. It is a challenge to all the actors and institutions that make up the U.S. economy.

A. The Scope and Effects of Unemployment

The importance of this goal is evident from the harm caused by unemployment in the United States today. Despite the recent recovery from severe recession, at the end of September 1984 there were 8.5 million people in the United States looking for a job who could not find one. They represent 7.4 percent of the labor force, a percentage which does not take account of those who have become so discouraged that they have stopped looking for work.[2] Between 1950 and 1980 the annual unemployment rate exceeded this percentage only during the recession years of 1975 and 1976.[3] Earlier periods of economic recovery during these three decades brought unemployment rates down to the 3 percent to 4 percent range. More recent years have seen a trend toward higher levels of unemployment even in good times and toward acceptance of these levels both by the public and by professional economists.[4]

. . .

The moral unacceptability of current unemployment levels becomes vividly clear from an examination of the effects of joblessness on human dignity. The self-respect of the person who has lost or cannot find a job often suffers severe damage. The unemployed come often to feel that they are worthless, without a productive role in society, in part because of the pervasive tendency in our society to blame the unemployed for unemployment, an assessment they often internalize.[5] Each day and in scores of ways our society tells them, We don't need your talent, we don't need your initiative, we don't need you. Historical research indicates that very few people survive long periods of unemployment without some psychological damage even if they have enough funds to meet their needs.[6] Unemployment insurance can pay for food, clothing and shelter, but it cannot provide the sense of being productive or of supporting one's family and of contributing to society. As elusive as these elements of personal identity may be, they can have a powerful impact on how an individual reacts to holding, losing or never having a job. Also crucial is whether individuals have other ways of putting their abilities to use after losing their jobs. For those in fairly routine jobs emotional well-being seems more closely tied to bringing home a paycheck than it is for professionals and others in high-status positions.[7] The devastation of unemployment seems greatest among those with the fewest inner resources and the smallest number of other options for work.

. . .

This review strongly supports the conclusion that current levels of unemployment and their attendant costs are morally unjustified. As a nation we are confronted with an urgent challenge to increase employment opportunities for all. If every effort were now being made to create the jobs required, one might argue that the situation today is the best we can do. But such is not the case. The country is doing far less than it might to generate employment, and it shows no sign of making a full-scale commitment to this goal. As moral teachers our first responsibility is to call for a change of direction, for the formation of a new national consensus that overcoming unemployment is at the top of the country's economic agenda.

B. Causes and Cures: Competing Interpretations

The difficulty of achieving such a new national consensus is real. It derives in part from our blindness to the suffering of the unemployed, but this is not the sole explanation. It is also a consequence of conflicting interpretations of what causes unemployment and of what policy steps will actually improve the situation.

. . .

Reflection on these various explanations clearly indicates that unemployment is not a simple phenomenon with a single cause. Therefore no single all-purpose cure is available. This does not mean, however, that nothing can be done. As a nation the United States has had considerable experience in trying to generate jobs and reduce unemployment. From 1932 through 1943 the U.S. government undertook a range of work-relief and public-works programs that still hold some lessons for the present.[8] More recently the federal government sponsored such initiatives as the Comprehensive Employment and Training Act, the Neighborhood Youth Corps, the Work Incentives Program, the New Jobs Tax Credit and its successor, the Targeted Jobs Tax Credit. In addition much can be learned from the many programs undertaken by local communities, business firms and private non-profit organizations to promote employment. Successes and failures have marked all these efforts. We wish to present several criteria drawn from reflection on past efforts which can help shape an effective response today.

First, attention must be sharply focused on the purpose of actually helping the unemployed. Well-intentioned programs in either the private or public sector which end up supporting jobs that would have existed anyway or which simply displace the burden of unemployment from one group of persons to another can hardly be called successful.[9] This means that job-generation efforts should aim specifically at bringing marginalized persons into the labor force and at the greatest *net* increase in the number of jobs. From both an economic and a moral perspective it is a waste of funds to make substantial investments in employment-generation activities whose yield of new jobs for those who are jobless will be small. Though this criterion may seem a truism, it has not always guided the policies of past or present job programs.

Second, the goal of employment policies should be long-term rather than short-term jobs. There are obvious advantages in policies leading to a greater number of regular jobs, whether in the private or public sector, as distinct from transitional jobs that are phased out when economic conditions improve. We would include under the rubric of regular, long-term employment those jobs created directly or indirectly by public investment for specific purposes, such as the rebuilding of roads, bridges and harbors. These should have priority over public investment in short-term employment creation during cycles of economic decline. Such short-term jobs obviously help those who hold them, but far less than relatively stable positions would do. Of even more limited value are subsidy schemes that encourage employers to take in workers for a limited period, such as one year, and then release them so that they can obtain additional benefits from a new set of workers.[10]

Third, the jobs created by employment programs should produce goods and services valued and needed by society. The design of job-creation programs should be clear on this point for many reasons, including responsibility in the use of funds and the need to gain public support. Nothing will undercut public commitment to employment generation more quickly than the perception that the main result is "leaf raking" or some other "make-work" of little value. Jobs that address a clear social need will not only make a productive contribution to society, but will also attract much wider public support. This criterion is relevant in both the private and public sectors.

Fourth, employment programs that generate jobs efficiently without entailing large expense and increased inflation should be emphasized. In our judgment the cost of programs and their effect on inflation should not be the sole or even the overriding criteria in deciding on jobs policies. The side effects of different employment programs on interest rates, public debt and inflation must, however, be considered in deciding which programs will be pursued. Government debt and U.S. interest rates affect domestic welfare; they also influence loan-repayment problems in many developing countries, particularly those in Latin America. High U.S. interest rates harm the poor in other parts of the world, who may have to give up basic necessities so that their governments can meet payments to U.S. banks. This linkage between the U.S. economy and the international economic order is an inescapable reality. The criterion suggested here, however, should be viewed as an aid to deciding *among* possible jobs programs and not as a reason for simply opposing them.

Fifth, an effective approach to unemployment calls for significant steps in both the private and public sectors, with joint action in both sectors at all levels of society. Enterprise, entrepreneurship and initiative are essential to the task of creating new jobs. The private sector accounts for about 80 percent of the jobs in the United States, and most new jobs are being created there as well.[11] A viable strategy for employment generation must assume that a large part of the solution will be with private firms and small businesses. But government also has a legitimate and necessary role to play, in particular by stimulating, coordinating and regulating initiatives for job generation. Tax policies, the allocation of credit and other supportive services should be shaped to help ensure the stability of small businesses and other new enterprises that provide needed jobs. Ideological disputes between those who believe the solution to lie solely with the private sector and those who would rely solely on government appear to us to be fruitless. In fact they can be harmful if they distract the nation from taking those steps which address the problem cooperatively. Successful long-range policies will require initiatives in both the private and public sectors, as well as joint action between them.

These criteria derive from the fundamental moral conviction of the Catholic tradition that employment should be available to all who seek it and from reflections on past efforts in the United States to achieve this objective. They do not solve every problem that will arise. We believe, however, that they point the way to a creative and realistic approach to policy which is rooted in respect for human dignity, solidarity and justice.

IV. POVERTY

The extent of poverty in the United States must be a matter of grave concern to all citizens. At the end of 1983 there were about 35 million Americans who, by the government's official definition, were poor. Another 20 million to 30 million had so little that by any reasonable standard they were also needy. After a decline in the annual rate of poverty from 14.7 percent in 1966 to 11.7 percent in 1979, the figure climbed to 15.2 percent by the end of 1983—the sharpest increase since poverty statistics began to be collected. In the four years between 1979 and 1983 the number of those living in poverty increased by over 9 million people.[1] During this same period the number of poor children under the age of 6 jumped by 51 percent.[2] The fact that so many people are poor in a nation as wealthy as ours is a social and moral scandal that must not be ignored.

These figures tell only part of the story of hardship in this country. One need look no further than our major cities to see examples of homelessness and hunger. Poor people, including many former mental patients released from state hospitals, roam the streets ill-clad and sleep in doorways or on subway grates at night. No one knows how many homeless people we now have, but estimates run from 250,000 to 3 million.[3] The striking rise in poverty has also led to problems for many in obtaining enough food. In the early 1980s the numbers of people seeking emergency food aid went up dramatically at agencies which provide such assistance.[4] Newspapers regularly chronicle the details of human beings forced to stand in line at soup kitchens because they have no other way of feeding themselves. The effects of improper nutrition are particularly damaging to small children, whose growth may be stunted and whose mental development may be impaired. In late 1983 the Massachusetts Department of Public Health reported that nearly one in five of the low-income children it surveyed was either stunted, abnormally underweight or anemic.[5] Similar studies in other areas have found comparable results. We believe that as a matter of justice the misery wrought by poverty in this country should be remedied as soon as possible.

A. Characteristics of Poverty

Poverty is an evil that strikes some groups more than others. In any given year the poor are most likely to be women, blacks, Hispanics, children, the elderly or handicapped. Perhaps most distressing is the fact that nearly half of all poor people are children. Today one in every four American children under the age of 6, and one in every two black children under 6, is poor. Most families with poor children receive no governmental assistance, have no health insurance and lack the funds to pay medical bills. Less than half are immunized against preventable diseases such as diphtheria and polio.[6]

Recent studies show that in the course of a decade nearly a quarter of the U.S. population will be in poverty at some time and will receive welfare benefits in at least one year. But the poor are not a stable group over time. People move into and out of poverty in response to such conditions as divorce and marriage, finding or losing a job, the death of a spouse or physical disability. Being poor is not limited to a dependent underclass or specific groups in the United States; it is a condition experienced at some time by people in many walks of life.[7]

While many of the poor manage to escape from beneath the official poverty line, others remain in poverty for extended periods of time.[8] One-third of this group is made up of elderly people who are typically not in a position to increase their income. Long-term poverty is also concentrated among blacks, and especially among families headed by black women. Blacks make up about 12 percent of the entire population but 62 percent of the persistently poor. Also striking is the extent of long-term poverty among families headed by women. Although only 19 percent of the population live in such families, they make up 61 percent of the persistently poor. People in this situation are also more likely to be from rural than from urban areas and from the South rather than from the North. In short, the long-term poor are disproportionately black, elderly, in families headed by women, from rural areas or small towns, and from the South. Most are either working at wages too low to bring them above the poverty line or are retired, disabled or parents of preschool children. Few are in a position to work more hours than they do now.[9]

. . .

One much-discussed condition that does not appear to be either a cause or a cure of poverty is personal motivation. Some claim that the poor are poor because they do not try hard enough to find a job, do not work hard enough when they have one and generally do not try to get ahead. In fact, one of the most detailed studies ever done on poverty in this country showed that initial attitudes were not an important predictor of later income.[10] Indeed, some of those who worked the longest hours remained poor because of low wages. Until there is real evidence that motivation significantly contributes to poverty, this kind of argument should be abandoned. It is not only unsupported but is insulting to the poor.

B. Social and Institutional Factors

Here we cannot enter into a full discussion of the nature of poverty, but we want to raise a few central points. Poverty is not merely the lack of adequate

financial resources. To be poor entails a more profound kind of deprivation, for it means being denied
full participation in the economic, social and political
life of society. It means being without sufficient control over and access to the decisions that affect your
life. It means being marginalized and powerless in a
way that assaults not only your pocketbook but also
your fundamental human dignity.

Our nation's response to poverty, therefore, must
not only include improvements in welfare programs
for the poor, as we shall discuss below. It must also
address broader social and institutional factors that are
an integral part of this problem. We call attention
here to three such factors: 1) racial discrimination; 2)
the feminization of poverty; and 3) the distribution of
income and wealth.

1. Racial and Ethnic Discrimination
As we indicated, the rates of poverty in this country
are highest among those groups that have historically
borne the brunt of racial prejudice and discrimination.
For example, blacks are about three times more likely
to be poor than whites. While one out of every eight
white Americans is poor, one of every three blacks
and more than one of every four Hispanics and Native
Americans is poor.[11] Black family income is only 55
percent of white family income, reflecting an income
gap that is wider than at any time in the 1970s.[12]

Racial prejudice in economic, social and political
structures continues to exclude non-whites from the

mainstream of American economic life. For example, discriminatory practices in labor markets, in educational systems and in electoral politics contribute to a severe and dangerous socio-economic gap between white and non-white America.

2. Feminization of Poverty

The past 20 years have witnessed a dramatic increase in the feminization of poverty. Between 1960 and 1980 the number of U.S. families headed by women rose 80 percent. At the same time there was a significant increase in the percentage of female-headed families living in poverty. As a result, families with female heads now have a rate of poverty six times that of two-parent families, while minority families supported by women have even higher rates.[13]

Many women are employed but are still poor because their wages are low. In 1978 more than 25 percent of the mothers who were working outside their homes and who headed households with children had incomes below the poverty level. More generally, women who work outside their homes full time and year-round earn only 61 percent of what men earn. It is thus clear that simply being employed full time is by itself not a remedy for poverty among women. Hundreds of thousands of women both hold full-time jobs and are still poor.

The causes of poverty for women differ in some ways from those for men. Despite the many changes in marriage and family life in recent decades, women

continue to have primary responsibility for childrear-
ing. When marriages are disrupted, mothers typically
take custody of the children and bear financial responsibility for supporting them. In 1981, of those eligible
for child support, only 35 percent received any payments; and those payments averaged only $2,110 per
year.[14]

Women often anticipate that they will leave the
labor force to have and raise children, and often make
job and career choices accordingly. Once they enter
the labor market, even women without children find
opportunities limited by their gender. Sixty percent
of all women work in only 10 occupations, and most
new jobs for women are in areas with low pay and
limited chances of advancement. In addition, women
suffer outright discrimination in wages, salaries, job
classifications, promotions and other areas. As a result,
they find themselves in jobs that have low pay and
status, little security, weak unionization, few fringe
benefits and not much intrinsic work satisfaction. If
they happen to be black, Hispanic or Native American, their situation is even worse.

*   *   *

C. Norms for Action
As we move to a discussion of measures to deal with
poverty and powerlessness in the United States, it is
important to keep in mind several of the relevant
moral themes that were explored in Part 1 of this
letter. The themes of human dignity and the preferential option for the poor characterize our approach to

the issue of poverty and compel us to confront it with a real sense of urgency. Dealing with poverty is not a luxury to which our nation can attend when it finds the time and resources. Rather, it is an imperative of the highest priority. It represents a strong moral claim on all of us.

The norms of social solidarity and participation convince us that the most appropriate and fundamental solutions to poverty will be those that support human dignity and enable people to take control of their own lives. This will require not only personal conversion but also fundamental changes in the institutions and structures of our society that perpetuate severe inequalities, that marginalize millions of citizens and prevent their full participation in the economic and social life of the nation.

. . .

1. A key element in removing poverty is prevention through a healthy economy.

The first lines of attack against poverty, as already noted, must be to build a healthy economy that provides employment opportunities at a decent wage for all adults who are able to work. Expanded employment would promote human dignity, increase social solidarity and be a source of self-reliance for the poor. It would also reduce the need for welfare programs and generate the income necessary to support those who remain in need, such as the elderly and disabled, the chronically ill and single parents who are unable to work. In this context it should be noted that while job creation and economic growth are major elements of a national strategy against poverty, they are clearly not enough. Other more specific policies are necessary to deal with the institutional causes of poverty and to provide for those who are unable to work.

2. Vigorous action should be undertaken to remove barriers to full and equal employment for women and minorities.

Our society needs to change the existing pattern in which women and minorities are locked into jobs with low pay, poor working conditions and little opportunity for career advancement. So long as this country tolerates a situation in which people can work full time and still be below the poverty line—a situation common among those earning the minimum wage—we will continue to have many members of the "working poor." Strong efforts must be made through job training and other means to assist those now blocked to obtain the more lucrative jobs.

3. Reforms in the tax system should be implemented that would reduce the burden on the poor.

We recognize the extreme complexities of tax policy and do not wish to offer extensive policy suggestions in this area. We do urge, however, that two principles be incorporated in any proposed tax reform. First, such reforms should eliminate or offset the payment of taxes by the poor. In recent years the total amount of taxes has increased substantially for the poor, while those at the top of the income scale have received significant reductions. Families below the official poverty line are, by definition, without sufficient resources to purchase the basic necessities of life. They should not be forced to bear the additional burden of paying federal taxes.

Second, we urge that the principle of progressivity be a central guiding norm in any forms of the tax system. Those with relatively greater financial resources should pay a higher rate of taxation. The inclusion of such a principle in tax policies is an important means of redressing the severe inequalities of income and wealth in the nation.

4. Government programs and policies
should stimulate and foster self-help
programs among the poor.

We believe that an effective way to attack poverty is through economic and human-development programs that are small in scale, locally based and oriented toward empowering the poor to become self-sufficient. Through partnerships with local private groups, the public sector can provide seed money, training and technical assistance, and organizational support for self-help projects in a wide variety of areas such as low-income housing, credit unions, worker cooperatives, legal assistance, and neighborhood and community organizations.

5. Schools should adopt policies leading to higher quality education for poor children.

Any long-term solution to the problem of poverty in this country must pay serious attention to education. There is now convincing evidence that schools could do more to increase learning among needy children.[15] Promising steps include more effective leadership by principals; greater expectations that *all* children can master a minimum amount of material; a clearer focus of instruction in the classroom; and evaluations based on specific measures of student achievement. In certain areas much more could be done to provide individual help for children who suffer from learning disabilities or other handicaps. Some of these reforms may require significant new expenditures, but others can be brought about even within existing systems. Improved education is no panacea for poverty's many disadvantages, but it is a good place to begin.

In this same spirit, we challenge our Catholic schools to remain in poor areas and to become models of education for the poor. They have already made many contributions, but they should continue to strive to provide the best possible education for the poor they serve. As bishops we pledge ourselves to support that effort.

. . .

D. Welfare Reform

We have emphasized that social welfare programs are no substitute for the fundamental reforms in social and economic policy that are necessary to empower the poor, to provide jobs at decent wages and to reduce the growing inequities in America's economic life. Nevertheless, for millions of poor Americans the only economic safety net is the public welfare system. We believe that programs in this area are essential and should be designed to serve the needs of the poor in a manner that respects their human dignity. In our judgment the present welfare system does not meet that criterion and is in need of major reform.

The United States has numerous separate programs to assist the needy, including four with broad coverage: Aid to Families with Dependent Children, Supplemental Security Income, food stamps and Medicaid, which provides certain health services to some of the poor. In general our welfare system is woefully inadequate. It is a patchwork arrangement marked by benefit levels that leave recipients poor; gaps in coverage; inconsistent treatment of poor people in similar situations; wide variations in benefits across states; humiliating treatment of clients; and frequent complaints about "red tape."

An unfair and unfortunate stereotype would have us believe that people receiving welfare benefits are persistently dependent on that source of income, are not working, could work if they wanted to and have children who will also be on welfare. This caricature is then used to argue against massive "welfare dependency" and for some version of "workfare." The present welfare system is also blamed for encouraging divorce, separation and illegitimate births.

The first obligation of citizens in debating public policy is to be aware of the relevant facts. In few areas is misinformation and misrepresentation as rampant as in discussions of welfare. Careful research shows that over a 10-year period welfare assistance is not limited to the same population of recipients. In fact, between 1969 and 1978 one-fourth of the American population lived in families receiving welfare in at least one year.[16] Nor is there any evidence of extensive long-term dependency on welfare benefits. While a quarter of the population lived in families receiving such benefits at some time, less than 1 percent obtained welfare income for all 10 years between 1969 and 1978. In other words, over a decade many families will receive welfare assistance at some point, but typically for a limited period of time. In about half the cases welfare is used to dig out of a crisis caused by divorce, job loss or the death of a spouse.[17] When the crisis ends, so does welfare. And, contrary to popular imagination, welfare dependency does not seem to pass from one generation to the next. Most children from welfare families do not themselves receive welfare, and most of those receiving welfare do not come from homes that had previously received such benefits.[18]

One reason why we do not have a humane welfare system is our punitive attitude toward the poor. Americans have a tendency to blame poverty on laziness, to stigmatize welfare recipients, to exaggerate the benefits actually received by the poor and to overstate the extent of fraud in welfare payments.[19] The belief persists in this country that the poor are poor by choice, that anyone can escape poverty by hard work and that welfare programs make it easier for people to avoid work. Hence we devise programs that single out the poor for special treatment, provide meager benefits and are often demeaning in the way they are administered. In violation of the spirit of solidarity, the needy are kept at the edge of society and told in dozens of ways that they are a burden. In this climate, politicians often find that they can score points by producing cuts in welfare programs, even when the cost is a sharp increase in human misery.

· · ·

Programs for the poor and the poor themselves also suffer from other myths. It is often alleged, for instance, that the rolls of AFDC are filled with able-bodied adults who could work but will not. In fact, most AFDC recipients are young children and their mothers, most of whom cannot work. These mothers are also accused of having more children so that they can raise their allowances. The truth is that 70 percent of AFDC families have only one or two children, and that there is little financial advantage in having another.[20] It is a basic moral obligation for citizens to avoid the stereotyping seen in these and similar myths.

· · ·

V. FOOD AND AGRICULTURE

U.S. agriculture is currently in a period of rapid and fundamental change. That change has long-term causes which can in large part be found in the industrialization and internationalization of the nation's economy, topics which have been addressed in other parts of this pastoral letter. Industrialization has made available to farmers new technologies involving large-scale equipment and the use of petroleum fuels. Internationalization has encouraged specialization in the foods farmers produce as other countries have become major consumers of U.S. grain and major sources of the fruits and vegetables consumed here. American agriculture is thus affected in significant ways by fluctuations in other sectors of the national economy and by shifts in international fiscal, political and market conditions.

The transformation brought about by changes in the farm economy carries with it consequences that are observable today in a particularly dramatic way as farm bankruptcies and foreclosures reach record levels.[1] Many farm families are losing inherited lands and are being driven out of a way of life that has held meaning for them and has served their local communities for generations. As these farm businesses close, other rural businesses and farm suppliers lose customers and jobs and rural communities further lose the tax base needed to provide basic services.

The current economic and social stress being felt in

farm communities reflects an acceleration of trends that have been occurring in the farm sectors since the 1940s.[2] The structures through which food, the most fundamental of all human needs, is produced and distributed have evolved significantly from what they were nearly 50 years ago. That evolution has had profound consequences for farm people and urban consumers, for rural communities and American society as a whole.

· · ·

Today nearly half of U.S. food production comes from the 4 percent of farms with over $200,000 in sales.[3] A small but increasing number of these largest farms are no longer operated by families but are owned by investors and managed by hired workers.[4] At the same time there is a large number of comparatively small farms, comprising nearly three-quarters of all farms, which account for only 13 percent of total farm sales. These farms are often run by part-time operators who derive most of their income from off-farm employment. The remaining 39 percent of sales come from the 24 percent of farms having $40,-000 to $200,000 in sales. These "moderate-sized" farms, generally owned and operated by full-time farm families, are the remnant of the traditional family farm system in the United States.

It is this group of family farmers who are at the center of the present farm "crisis." They are facing economic conditions which further accelerate long-term trends toward fewer and larger farms. For decades federal tax policies and farm programs supporting the prices of certain commodities and protecting farm earnings have encouraged the investment of capital in agriculture.[5] Increased borrowing by farmers served to speed the adoption of costly technologies and the expansion of farms into larger units. During the 1970s new markets for farm exports created additional opportunities for profits in agriculture, stimulated greater production and added to the value of farm land. Many farmers borrowed heavily to finance expansion and then were unable to repay their loans when in the 1980s export markets dried up and commodity prices and land values declined.

This recent experience is in part a consequence of a unique combination of circumstances in the economies of the United States and the world. These circumstances include peristent high interest rates, the high value of the dollar, reduced international trade as a result of the global recession, dramatically higher U.S. budget and trade deficits, and the massive and growing debt burden of food-importing developing countries. With the resulting decline in grain exports and the buildup of price-depressing agricultural surpluses, farm income dropped and many farms became financially insolvent.

The human suffering involved in the present situation calls for a compassionate response by the rest of society. More than that, however, it calls attention to the broader implications of these long-term trends.[6]

· · ·

A. Guidelines for Action

The decline in the number of moderate-sized farms and evidence of poor resource conservation raise serious questions of morality and public policy. As pastors we cannot stand by while thousands of farm families caught in the present crisis lose their homes, their land and their way of life. We approach this situation, however, aware that it reflects longer-term conditions which hold implications for the food system as a whole and for the land, water and energy resources essential for food production. We are convinced that current trends are not the only ones possible. Moreover they do not appear to us to be in the best interests of our nation and the global community.

. . .

First, moderate-sized farms operated by families on a full-time basis should be preserved and their economic viability protected. One reason for this is that there is real value in maintaining a wide distribution in the ownership of productive property. As we have noted elsewhere in this pastoral letter, the church has long defended this value. When those who work in an enterprise also share in its ownership, their active participation in the endeavor is enhanced. Ownership provides incentives for diligence and is a source of an increased sense that the work being done is truly one's own. This is particularly significant in a sector as vital to human well-being as is agriculture. Farms of moderate size are usually operated by the owners of the land and their family members, who take pride in working the land and cherish both their independence and their sense of making a distinctive contribution to the comunity. The democratization of decision making and control of the land inherent in such a wide distribution of farm-land ownership is a protection against concentration of power and a possible loss of responsiveness to public need in this crucial sector of the economy.

Another reason for the importance of maintaining moderate-sized farms is that diversity in farm ownership prevents excessive dependence on large-scale enterprises that make business decisions primarily on the basis of their impact on the rate of return to invested capital. The very large farms, already responsible for nearly half of the country's agricultural production, will continue to have a role in American agriculture. Allowing them to become the primary source of the country's food, however, would make our food system overly susceptible to fluctuations in the market for investment capital. This is particularly true in the case of non-farm corporations that enter agriculture to get a high return on investment. If that return drops substantially or if it appears to stockholders and management that better returns can be obtained by investing the same capital in other sectors, they may cut back or even close down their operations without regard to the impact on the community or the food system.

·   ·   ·

The quality of rural life has a value beyond the rural community itself. Both Catholic social teaching and the traditions of our country have emphasized the value of maintaining a rich plurality of social institutions that enhance personal freedom and increase the opportunity for participation in community life. Movement toward a small number of very large farms employing many wage workers would be a movement away from this institutional pluralism. By contributing to the vitality of rural communities, full-time residential farmers enrich the social and political life of the nation as a whole.

Second, the opportunity to engage in farming should be protected as a valuable form of employment. At a time when unemployment in the country is already too high, any unnecessary loss of jobs in agriculture should be avoided. Full-time work in farming provides a way of life that rural people want to preserve and that is valuable to society as a whole. The loss of people from the land means the loss of expertise in farm and land management. It also creates a need for retraining and relocating of those who have been displaced.

. . .

Third, stewardship of the natural endowment should be a central consideration in any measures impacting on U.S. agriculture. Such stewardship is a contribution to the common good that is difficult to assess in purely economic terms because it involves the care of resources given by our Creator for the benefit of all, including future generations. The responsibility for the stewardship of natural resources rests on society as a whole. Since they make their living from the use of this endowment, however, farmers bear a particular obligation to be good stewards of land and water. They fulfill this obligation by participating in soil and water conservation programs, using farm practices that are not damaging to land or water, and maintaining farmland in food production rather than converting it to non-farm uses. Like all efforts to protect the environment, soil and water conservation are contributions to the good of the whole society. It is thus appropriate for the public to bear a share of the cost of these practices and to set standards for environmental protection.

B. Policies and Actions

In view of these guidelines and the importance we attach to the family farm, we urge that governmental interventions in the farm sector be redirected to give first priority to small and moderate-sized farms. A half century of federal farm price supports, subsidized credit, production-oriented research and extension services, and special tax policies for farmers have made the federal government a central factor in almost every aspect of American agriculture. No redirection of current trends can occur without giving close attention to these programs. At the same time the consequences of any significant or abrupt change in federal farm programs must be carefully considered.

The current crisis appears to us to call for special measures to assist viable family farms that are threatened with bankruptcy or foreclosure. Operators of such farms should have access to emergency credit and programs of debt restructuring. Local lending institutions facing problems because of non-payment or slow payment of large farm loans should also have access to temporary assistance. These and other short-term measures are fully justified by the expected gains for farmers and their families, their communities and the larger society. Keeping these people on the land will help to maintain a wider distribution of farm-land ownership, support the viability of rural communities and enhance the security and responsiveness of our food-production system. In addition to these immediate measures, established federal farm programs should be reassessed in view of their long-term effects on the structure of agriculture.

. . .

C. Conclusion

America's farm and food economy functions within the larger industrial and service economy of the nation. The very nature of agricultural enterprise and the family farm traditions of this country have kept this a highly competitive sector with a widely dispersed ownership of the most fundamental input to production, the land. That competitive, diverse structure, proven to be a dependable source of a secure and abundant supply of food, is now threatened by a combination of unfortunate economic circumstances and by trends in public policy. At risk are the food necessary for life, the land and water resources needed to produce that food and the way of life of the people who make the land productive. Catholic social and ethical traditions attribute moral significance to each of these. Our response to the present situation should reflect a sensitivity to that moral significance and an intention to leave to future generations an enhanced natural environment and the same ready access to the necessities of life that we enjoy today.

VI. A NEW AMERICAN EXPERIMENT: COLLABORATING TO SHAPE THE ECONOMY

These discussions of several key areas of U.S. economic policy reveal that we all face an enormous task. If our nation is to rise to the challenges before it, we shall have to see a significantly increased level of collaboration and cooperation among the many economic actors in our society. Joint effort and teamwork have been as much hallmarks of our country's history and culture as have personal initiative and a competitive spirit. This collaborative spirit needs to take on new life and new forms today if initiative and competition are going to serve the common good. A number of students of U.S. economic and political culture believe that the sense of being part of the commonweal and of having obligations as well as rights within it has grown weak. They identify this problem as a

crisis of citizenship—the loss of a vision of the good
of society as a whole.[1] When such a vision is lacking,
groups within our political economy that have particularly strong interests can exercise veto power over
policies essential to the protection of human dignity.[2]
Such power swells when the group that wields it
already possesses large economic resources.

To resist this danger we believe that America needs
a new experiment in cooperation and collaboration.
Such an experiment has a moral and cultural aspect:
the renewal and enhancement of the sense of solidarity
we have discussed above.[3] It will also call for political
and institutional innovations which enhance genuine
participation and broaden the sharing of responsibility
in economic society. In line with the principle of
subsidiarity discussed above, this collaboration should
occur in different ways on different levels of the
economy.[4] We want to suggest several directions in
which the economic life of the United States can
move that will increase cooperation and strengthen
mutual responsibility.

A. Cooperation Within Individual Firms and Industries
One of the most important means for enhancing this
spirit of cooperation is the development of a new
partnership between workers and managers. Both
labor and management suffer when adversary positions become extreme, as recent experience in a number of industries has shown. In fact the productivity
and success of any enterprise result from the joint

contribution of workers, managers and investors. As Pope Leo XIII stated, "Each needs the other completely: Capital cannot do without labor nor labor without capital."[5] Therefore the organization of these enterprises should reflect and enhance this mutual partnership.

First, support for a less adversarial relationship between labor and management does not mean that workers alone are called upon to make sacrifices. Real collaboration cannot occur where one of the contributing groups holds effective power exclusively or disproportionately. For example, agricultural workers, particularly migrant laborers, are already making contributions not reflected in their wages, benefits or bargaining power. In the heavy manufacturing sector of the U.S. economy technological change and international competition are pushing firms and industries toward very painful choices. We acknowledge that choices leading to job losses or wage reductions for workers may sometimes be necessary. But a collaborative and mutually accountable model of industrial organization demands that workers not have to bear all the burdens of a dynamic economy in transition. Management and investors must also make their share of the sacrifices, especially, for example, when management is contemplating transferring capital to a potentially more productive or competitive location. The capital at the disposal of management represents to a significant degree the investment of the labor of those who have toiled in the company over the years, including currently employed workers.[6] It is patently unjust to deny these workers any role in shaping the outcome of such difficult choices.[7] As a minimum, workers have a right to be informed in advance when such decisions are under consideration, a right to negotiate with management about possible alternatives and a right to fair compensation and assistance with retraining and relocation expenses should these be necessary. Without collective negotiation even these minimal rights will be jeopardized, and so industrial cooperation requires a strong role for responsible labor unions in our changing economy. Also, the local communities in which these companies are located have often invested heavily in them through public services, tax benefits, public education and a host of other community resources. They too have a right to expect management to respect their investment.

Second, workers should organize not only to defend their basic rights, but also to fulfill their positive responsibilities to their employers and to the larger society.[8] If we seek greater justice, we need to explore new avenues of collaboration among labor, management, investors and local communities.

The challenge of working together for a more just economy should stimulate increased efforts by business and labor to develop new institutions of economic partnership in the United States. We believe such efforts will not only enhance solidarity within a given firm, but also promote a broader commitment to the common good of society as a whole.

B. Local and Regional Cooperation

Individual firms and indeed whole industries are not sole masters of their own fate. Local, regional, national and international conditions, both economic and political, have a major impact on particular economic enterprises. This means we need increased collaborative efforts to make these social contexts contribute to the goal of a more just economy.[9]

The value of collaboration in shaping policies on a local or regional basis is perhaps best illustrated in the generation of new jobs. As noted above, recent empirical research indicates that one of the keys to revitalizing areas hard hit by unemployment is the development of new businesses, especially smaller ones which account for the larger proportion of new jobs created in recent years.[10] The cities and regions in greatest need of these new jobs however, face serious obstacles in attracting enterprises that can generate them. Lack of financial resources, lower levels of entrepreneurial skill, blighted and unsafe environments and a deteriorating infrastructure create a vicious cycle which makes new investment in these areas more risky and therefore less likely. In the agricultural sector, the depletion of the land threatens not only jobs that already exist in farming but also prevents the creation of new jobs in this productive sector.

C. Cooperation in the Development of National Policies

Both the causes of our national economic problems and their possible solutions are the subject of vigorous debate today, and much of it turns on the role the national government has played in causing them and should play in responding to them. Our concern is not with adjudicating the complex economic aspects of this argument. We want instead to point to several considerations that should help build new forms of effective citizenship and cooperation to shape the economic life of our country.

First, while economic freedom, personal initiative and the free market are deservedly esteemed in our society, we have increasingly come to recognize the inescapably social and political nature of the economy. No market is ever free from the surrounding society. It is always embedded in a specific social and political context that impinges on economic relations. For example, the tax system is an obvious force that affects consumption, saving and investment. Other governmental actions also directly affect the market, as in the cases of national monetary policy and spending on both domestic and defense programs, regulation in the interests of environmental protection and worker safety, and tariffs and quotas on international trade. These policies influence domestic investment, unemployment rates, foreign exchange and the health of the entire world economy.

. . .

We are well aware that the mere mention of the notion of economic planning is likely to produce a violent allergic reaction in U.S. society. It conjures up images of centralized planning boards, command economies, inefficient bureaucracies, mountains of government paperwork and entangling skeins of red tape. We are also aware that the very meaning of the word "planning" is open to a wide array of interpretations and that economic planning takes very different forms in various nations.[11] In no way can the pope's words be construed as an endorsement of a highly centralized form of economic planning, much less a totalitarian one. Rather his call for a "just and rational coordination" of the endeavors of the many economic actors is a call to seek that balance between individual initiatives and the common good which is the responsibility of all citizens.

. . .

D. International Cooperation

The U.S. economy is linked with the rest of the world economy in multiple ways. Many of these links are of positive benefit both to the people of the United States and to those of other nations. It is also clear, however, that the present pattern does harm as well as good to large numbers of persons.

If we are to guide our international economic relationships by policies that serve human dignity and justice, we must first broaden our understanding of our own moral responsibility. Citizenship carries with it a vocation to serve the common good. Today that vocation extends to the service of the universal common good of the entire planet. Though national boundaries and national interest continue to have a legitimate meaning in a world of sovereign nation states, economic policy cannot be governed by national goals alone. The fact that the "social question has become worldwide"[12] challenges us to widen our horizons as U.S. citizens today. This challenge to enhance collaboration and mutual responsibility on a global level has been a constant theme of the teachings of recent popes and of the Second Vatican Council.[13] It calls for more extensive discussion in the following section of this letter.

VII. THE UNITED STATES AND THE WORLD ECONOMY: COMPLEXITY, CHALLENGE AND CHOICES

A. Economic Relations in an Interdependent World

Popes from Pius XII to John Paul II have given renewed emphasis to the traditional principles of Catholic teaching on interdependence: the dignity of the human person, the unity of the human family, the universally beneficial purpose of the goods of the earth, the need to pursue the international common good and the intensifying imperative of distributive justice in a world ever more sharply divided between rich and poor. "The scandal of the shocking inequality between the rich and the poor," the Vatican Congregation for the Doctrine of the Faith said Sept. 3, 1984, "—whether between rich and poor countries, or between social classes in a single nation—is no longer tolerated. On the one hand, people have attained an unheard-of abundance which is given to waste, while on the other hand so many live in such poverty, deprived of the basic necessities, that one is hardly able even to count the victims of malnutrition."[1] These basic tenets take on new moral urgency as we deepen our recognition of how interdependent the world is.

In that interdependent world the United States is still the economic giant—despite its own recent recession and the rise of other economic powers. The American economy has an enormous influence on the rest of the world, especially the developing countries; and those countries are increasingly important participants in international economic activity, with a growing impact on the United States. Such interdependence, as we emphasized earlier in this letter[2] and in our pastoral letter on war and peace, is central to any assessment of the role of the United States in the world. In recent years Catholic teaching in this area has focused more and more on this concept of interdependence and on the moral responsibility it brings with it.

. . . .

To return again to the central theme, interdependence is not evenhanded; the degree of dependency varies enormously, from that of the relatively independent superpowers to that of landlocked developing nations totally dependent for foreign exchange upon earnings from the single agricultural or other commodity they export. In certain respects the relationship between developing countries and industrialized countries resembles the interdependence, respectively, of horse and rider.

B. The Relevance of Catholic Social Teaching

We are talking about people—each of them uniquely created by God in his image and endowed with the same rights as readers of this letter. They are at risk in our interdependent world, and our understanding of their jeopardy forces on us the moral significance of interdependence. Our challenge is to choose community over chaos, to go beyond the neutrality of fact and to shape the conditions of interdependence according to standards of justice, equity and charity. We want a world that works fairly for all. Effective action toward this end requires a definition of political community that, while acknowledging national sovereignty, also recognizes political and moral bonds among nations and across national boundaries that must influence public policy.

In this arena of policy, where the factual and the moral challenges of interdependence intersect, the moral task is to devise rules to govern the activities of three key sets of actors:

First, though individual nations are no longer the only actors affecting the international environment, their policies remain the most influential. They continue to stress their independence and sovereignty, but they act today in a setting shaped by the fact of interdependence. Policies that disregard it will not work. The multilateral institutions that serve as key structures of the international economic system—the World Bank, the regional development banks,[3] the International Monetary Fund and the U.N. agencies —are a *second* important set of actors, channeling money, power, ideas and influence. These countries and institutions share the global stage today with a *third* set of transnational actors, principally transnational corporations engaged in manufacturing, trade and finance, which have increased dramatically in number, size, scope and power since World War II.[4] Their wealth, technology, clarity of purpose, capacity to operate across national and ideological lines—and their sheer size[5]—make them major factors in the functioning of an interdependent world, outstripping most nations and multilateral agencies in their ability to manage activities on a global scale.[6]

. . .

Catholic teaching on the international economic order fully recognizes the complexity of interdependence, but it sees its main contribution as ensuring that moral considerations are not left out of the policy debate. For guidance on this score three key themes emerge from recent papal teaching: *the need for reform of the international system, the need to refashion national policies and the acceptance of a "preferential option for the poor" as an overall policy imperative.* Proposals for basic reform of the international economic system that has been in place since the end of World War II fill the policy literature today. Though differing greatly in content, these proposals often start from the same premise: the need for a fundamental recasting, not simply a modification, of the present system.[7] Catholic teaching, which posits an international order structured to respect human dignity and achieve equity, reflects a similar call for basic reform. Whether the question is preventing war and building peace, or addressing the needs of the developing nations, Catholic teaching emphasizes not only the individual conscience, but also the political, legal and economic structures through which policy is determined and issues adjudicated.

. . .

We do not intend to evaluate the various proposals for international economic reform or to provide a blueprint for a new international system. Rather we want to urge a basic and overriding consideration: that both empirical and moral evidence, especially the precarious situation of the developing countries, calls for the renewal of the dialogue urged by Pope John Paul II between North and South.[8] *We strongly recommend that such a dialogue aim at restructuring the existing patterns of economic relations so as to establish greater equity and meet the basic human needs of the poor people of the South.*

. . .

To make the assessment of which Pope Paul VI spoke, a third principle from current Catholic teaching needs to be invoked—what we have described in this letter as the *preferential option for the poor.* This principle provides a unique perspective on foreign policy from which U.S.-developing country relationships can be judged. Standard foreign-policy analysis deals with calculations of power and definitions of national interest. But the poor are, almost by definition, not powerful. If we are to weigh their concerns, their needs and how their interests relate to this nation's interest, we must go beyond a conventional economic or strategic starting point for policy. We want to stand with the poor everywhere, and *we urge that U.S.-developing world relations should be determined in the first place by a concern for the basic human needs of the poor.*

C. U.S. International Development Policy: A Critique
In recent years U.S. policy toward the developing world has shifted from its earlier emphasis on basic human needs and social and economic development to a selective assistance based on an East-West assessment of a North-South set of problems. Such a view makes the principal policy issue one of "national security," which in turn is described in political-military terms.[9] Developing countries thus become largely test cases in the East-West struggle; they have meaning or value only in terms of the larger geopolitical calculus. The result is that issues of political and economic development take second place to the political-strategic argument. We deplore this change.

. . .

We believe that in terms of perspective, policy and posture there is urgent need for a change in the U.S. approach to these negotiations and to developing countries. We make this assertion out of the conviction that a country of our size, resources and potential has a moral obligation to help reduce poverty in the Third World. Moreover, we believe that our present posture and policy do not reflect either the best traditions of our history or the best values that the American people hold. We know from our pastoral work that Americans are a generous, compassionate people. Our policies should reflect our best instincts; currently they do not.

D. The United States and Developing Countries: Constructive Choices

The redirection of U.S. policy toward the developing world should reflect in international relations our traditional regard for human rights and our attention to social progress on the national level. In economic policy alone, as we noted in our pastoral letter on war and peace, the major relationships of trade, aid, finance and investment are both interdependent among themselves and illustrative of the range of interdependence issues facing U.S. policy.[10] Each offers the United States the possibility of a substantial, positive response which could signal a fundamental change of attitude in the direction of increasing social justice in the developing world.

1. Trade Relations

International trade has been and continues to be an essential component of economic progress for the developing countries. It contributed in a major way to their rapid growth in the 1960s and 1970s, and it promises to be an at least equally important element in the 1980s and 1990s.[11] For the industrialized countries too, trade represents an aspect of interdependence; for example, about 40 percent of U.S. exports of manufactured goods go to Third-World countries; one out of every eight jobs depends on exports; and one out of every three acres of cultivated land produces for foreign markets (more than half of this for the Third World).[12] Any realistic appraisal of the role of developing countries in the world economy suggests that their importance will continue to grow and that for the foreseeable future they will import more than they export. At the same time, when we see the disadvantageous terms of trade[13] under which the developing countries operate (their imports cost them far more than their exports can earn), we come to the same conclusion that prompted Pope Paul VI to describe international trade as the testing ground of social justice for the developing countries.[14]

. . .

We believe the ethical norms we have applied to domestic economic questions[15] are equally valid here. The United States must do all it can to ensure that the poorest segments of developing countries' societies benefit fairly from the trading system and that U.S.

workers and families affected by that system be helped through training and other measures to adjust to changed conditions.

We would also emphasize that trade policy alone, however enlightened, is not a sufficient approach toward the developing countries. It must be joined with finance, aid and investment policies.

2. Third-World Debt

. . .

For the richer debtor countries, on the other hand, what is needed is an equitable adjustment process that does not penalize the poor. Although the ultimate policy decisions about the allocation of adjustments belong to the debtor government, we believe that the IMF could take some of these equity considerations into account in determining conditionality, e.g., by not insisting on reducing wages. We believe the United States should take the lead in urging such modification.

3. Development Assistance

The third major resource transfer from the industrialized to the developing countries, "foreign aid," gets an increasingly bad press in the United States. Everyone remembers the Marshall Plan, which helped rebuild devastated, but sophisticated, economic structures in Europe and Japan; later efforts at foreign aid, which have tried to help countries build economies where there was little such structure, inevitably suffer by comparison. Thus in the 1980s few public figures in our nation are willing even to talk about foreign aid, except perhaps in the security context we have described. Its supporters seem paralyzed intellectually and politically. The reasons for this reluctance are many: Some arise out of U.S. politics, some out of U.S. disenchantment with "ungrateful" Third-World aid recipients, some out of fatigue and frustration at the apparently endless nature of what was thought to be a "temporary" program. But whatever the difficulties, the need for assistance to the developing world is undeniable; and the cost of not providing it can be counted in human lives lost or stunted, talents wasted, opportunities foregone, suffering and misery prolonged, and injustice condoned.

. . . .

E. U.S. Responsibility for Reforms in the International Economic Order

Trying to deal with all the vast array of international economic problems would turn this letter into a treatise on global development—something we have no intention of doing. Nor do we believe the United States can be the sole savior of the developing world or that Third-World countries are entirely innocent with respect to their own failures or helpless to achieve their own destinies. Progress toward development will require Third-World governments to curtail spending on inefficient public enterprises, to reduce borrowing, to streamline bureaucracies and to take very difficult steps toward empowering their people. Still, the pervasive presence of U.S. power in many parts of our interdependent world creates a responsibility to use that power in the service of human dignity and human rights—both political and economic.[16] In particular, as we have noted in our previous letter, the relationship between expenditures on armaments and on development points to a massive distortion of resources. In 1982 the military expenditures of the developed countries were 17 times larger than their foreign assistance; in 1984 the United States alone budgeted more than 20 times as much for defense as for foreign assistance[17] and nearly two-thirds of the latter took the form of military assistance or went to countries because of their perceived security value to the United States. *Rather than promoting U.S. arms sales to countries that cannot afford them, we should be campaigning for an international agreement to reduce this lethal trade.*

. . .

To restructure the international order along lines of greater equity and participation will require a far more stringent application of the principles of affirmative action than we have seen in the United States itself. Like the struggle for political democracy at home, it will entail sacrifices. But that is what the recognition and acceptance of responsibility means. As a nation founded on Judeo-Christian religious principles, we are called to make those sacrifices in order to bring justice and peace to the world, as well as for our own long-term self-interest. The times call for the kinds of leadership and vision that have characterized our nation in the past when the choices were clear. Now we need to call upon these qualities again. As Pope John Paul II said to President Carter during his visit to the United States, "America, which in the past decades has demonstrated goodness and generosity in providing food for the hungry of the world, will, I am sure, be able to match this generosity with an equally convincing contribution to the establishing of a world order that will create the necessary economic and trade conditions for a more just relationship between all the nations of the world."[18]

. . . .

We recognize that we are dealing here with sensitive international issues that cross national boundaries. Nevertheless, in order to pursue justice and avoid that judgment, *we call for a U.S. international economic policy designed to empower people and give them a sense of their own worth, to help them improve the quality of their lives, and to ensure that the benefits of economic growth are shared equitably among them.*

CONCLUSION
A CALL TO WHOLENESS AND HOLINESS

This letter has addressed many questions about life in society which are commonly regarded as secular matters. Employment rates, income levels and international economic relationships are all clearly affairs of this world. The fact that our discussion of these topics has drawn heavily on the experience and knowledge of persons engaged in the daily affairs of economic life and on the writings of a variety of economists and social scientists bears witness to our conviction that earthly affairs have a rightful independence which the church and we as bishops must respect.[1] Within a context shaped by such respect we have also sought to uncover the moral and religious meaning of the urgent economic problems facing our country today. The Second Vatican Council eloquently described these fundamental questions men and women are asking today about their activity in the world, questions which cry out for deeper answers than secular experience and social science can provide:

"What is the meaning and value of this feverish activity? How should all these things be used? To the achievement of what goal are the strivings of individuals and societies heading? . . . What is this sense of sorrow, of evil, of death which continues to exist despite so much progress? What is the purpose of these victories, purchased at so high a cost? What can man offer to society, what can he expect from it? What follows this earthly life?"[2]

Such questions clearly indicate that affairs of the world, including economic ones, cannot be separated from the spiritual quest of the human heart. For this reason we have presented the church's moral and religious tradition as a framework for addressing the deeper questions about the meaning of economic activity and the active response which should flow from it.

· · ·

A. Labor and Leisure

Some of the difficulty in relating Christian faith to economic life in the United States today is the result of how hard it has become for many to establish a balance of labor and leisure in their lives. This problem takes a number of forms. Tedious and boring work leads some people to look for fulfillment only during time off the job. The pace of a high-speed technological society traps others into becoming "workaholics" who do not know how to stop their driven behavior long enough to ask why they are doing these things at all. Long-term unemployment creates a class of poor persons excluded from meaningful work and from the education and opportunity to share in the riches of culture. We do not expect the human condition to be relieved of the tension between toil and rest until the kingdom of God has been fully established at the end of days. Building both the pattern and the pace of work on a more human scale, however, will enable people to experience the value and dignity of their labor and give them time to reflect on the deeper questions of life's meaning. What we have said about increased participation in economic institutions can help bring this about. The kinds of leisure people enjoy also affect their ability to connect religious-moral values with economic life. Relaxed contemplation of the fruitfulness of the land and the beauty of God's creation helps us understand our ecological and agricultural responsibilities. The

theater, music and poetry of different national and
ethnic communities reveal how the same longing for
wholeness arises in the life of every human being. The
fiesta which is so important in Hispanic communities
shows that all of life—with its many sufferings and
its many joys—should lead us to communal celebration, which in turn builds up human solidarity.

B. Work and Worship

On another level, overcoming the split between the
Christian vision and economic life calls for a deeper
awareness in the church of the integral connection
between worship and the world of work. Worship
and prayer are the center of Christian existence and
the pre-eminent purpose of the church. They are also
the wellspring that gives life to our reflection on
economic problems. To worship God is to fall on
one's knees in awe and praise before the source and
creator of everything. It is to acknowledge that one
is a sinner in need of forgiveness and conversion. It
is to offer heartfelt thanks that in Jesus Christ God
continually extends that forgiveness and healing redemption to all creation. To worship the God of the
universe is to acknowledge that the creative, forgiv-
ing and healing love of God extends to all persons and
to every part of existence, including work, money,
economic power and the policies which either lead to
justice or impede it. Therefore, when Christians come
together in prayer and praise we make a commitment
to carry God's love into all these areas of life. True

holiness is not limited to the sanctuary or to moments of private prayer. It means being a disciple of Christ and seeing our use of the goods of the earth in the light of the gospel command to have a special concern for the poor and needy (Mt. 25:31–46).

The call to holiness is addressed to every Christian, in every walk of life. "The Lord Jesus, the divine teacher and model of all perfection, preached holiness of life to each and every one of his disciples regardless of their situation."[3] Sanctity is the vocation not only of bishops, priests and religious, but it is equally the call of parents, workers, business people and politicians.

.   .   .

This holiness is achieved in the midst of the world. In this letter we have repeatedly pointed out how the decisions of many economic actors and institutions profoundly affect the lives and well-being of millions of persons. The constant effort to shape these decisions and institutions in ways that enhance human dignity and reflect the grandeur and glory of God represents a most important path to holiness. Men and women in business, on farms, in factories, in government, in scientific and educational institutions, and in every other field of labor can achieve true sanctity when they respond to the call of discipleship in the midst of their work. The church in its ministry has a responsibility to nurture and sustain this response. Therefore, we urge dioceses, parishes, retreat houses and other appropriate church bodies to develop new and effective programs to support the spiritual development of lay persons, a development which will depend on authentic integration of work and worship. The church's ministry of aiding spiritual growth and fostering prayer and the ministry of promoting justice and peace must not be separated from each other. All engaged in these activities need to develop a deeper awareness of the unity of action and contemplation in the Christian life.[4]

.   .   .

Therefore we call on all Christians in the United States to seek that integral form of holiness to which the Gospel beckons, a holiness in which work and worship, economic life and Christian vision interpenetrate and constantly interact. Achieving this will demand prayer, reflection, study and action. We ask everyone to reflect on the contents of this letter and to attempt to apply it to the economic questions that confront our nation and our world. The rich resource of Catholic social teaching should animate the curricula of church-sponsored schools and adult-education programs. Parish and diocesan justice and peace agencies have a major role to play in aiding the Catholic community in the United States to listen and respond to the message of this letter. In a special way we challenge Catholic institutions of higher learning to increase their research and teaching in these areas, for we recognize that our own efforts are limited and but a beginning. The church as a whole needs the reflection and wisdom these institutions can uniquely provide. We commend the many groups who have already done so much to show us the way: the St. Vincent de Paul Society, the Catholic Worker movement, parish social-service groups, Catholic Charities agencies, justice and peace commissions, and many others who reflect the beauty of the holiness that grows through service of the poor. We want to renew our own initiatives, begun through the Campaign for Human Development, to find ways of empowering all persons to a fuller measure of participation in social life. We recommend personal sacrifices as well— almsgiving and direct service to the poor, for example —that can make these vast issues personal to each of us.

God has given us as a nation so very much. We are a generous people. But the moment has come to examine in greater depth the need for true justice in the economic sphere, so that the poor in our country and the peoples of all nations will benefit more fully from God's gifts. Our concern for economic justice for all has impelled us to make this study. It urges us to continue to make this concern the urgent task of the church in the United States and the concern of all people.

We wish, in the end, to go beyond the need to create a world in which economic justice abounds: We seek to be a part of a world where love and friendship among all citizens of the globe becomes the primary goal of all. In this love and friendship God is glorified and God's grandeur revealed.

FOOTNOTES

THE CHURCH AND THE ECONOMY: WHY WE SPEAK

[1] Vatican Council II, Pastoral Constitution on the Church in the Modern World, 1. Papal and conciliar texts will be referred to by title with paragraph number. Editions of some of these texts are published by the U.S. Catholic Conference Office of Publishing Services. Others are available in several collections, though no single collection is comprehensive. See the following: Leo XIII, *Rerum Novarum* ("On the Condition of Labor"), (Washington, D. C.: USCC, n.d.); Pius XI, *Quadragesimo Anno* ("On Reconstructing the Social Order"), (Washington, D. C.: USCC, n.d.); William J. Gibbons, ed., *Seven Great Encyclicals* (New York: Paulist Press, 1963); Joseph Gremillion, ed., *The Gospel of Peace and Justice: Catholic Social Teaching Since Pope John XXIII* (Maryknoll, N.Y.: Orbis Books, 1976); David J. O'Brien and Thomas A. Shannon, eds., *Renewing the Earth: Catholic Documents on Peace, Justice and Liberation* (Garden City, N.Y.: Doubleday, 1977); Austin P. Flannery, ed., *Vatican Council II: The Conciliar and Post Conciliar Documents* (Collegeville, Minn.: Liturgical Press, 1975); Walter M. Abbott and Joseph Gallagher, eds., *The Documents of Vatican II* (New York: America Press, 1966); John Paul II, "Redeemer of Man" *(Redemptor Hominis)* (Washington, D.C.: USCC, 1979); John Paul II, "On Human Work" *(Laborem Exercens)* (Washington, D.C.: USCC,

1981); John Paul II, "Rich in Mercy" *(Dives in Misericordia)* (Washington, D.C.: USCC, 1980); John Paul II, "On The Christian Meaning Of Human Suffering" *(Salvifici Doloris)* (Washington, D.C.: USCC, 1984). (In certain of the quotations from these documents in this letter the texts have been retranslated into language which is both faithful to the original and sexually inclusive.)

[2] Homily at Le Breton Flats, Sept. 20, 1984, in Origins, vol. 14: 16 (Oct. 4, 1984), p. 251.

I. CHRISTIAN VISION OF ECONOMIC LIFE

[1] See Gn. 1:26; Wis. 2:23; "Peace on Earth," 3; Pastoral Constitution, 12ff.

[2] See Pastoral Constitution, 22; "Redeemer of Man," 14.

[3] Pastoral Constitution, 24.

[4] On the importance of the covenant at Sinai to biblical ethics, see esp. T. W. Ogletree, *The Use of the Bible in Christian Ethics* (Philadelphia: Fortress Press, 1983), pp. 47–85.

[5] See C. Westermann, *Creation* (Philadelphia: Fortress, 1974) and B. Vawter, *On Genesis: A New Reading* (Garden City, N.Y.: Doubleday, 1977).

[6] Pastoral Constitution, 34.

[7] On justice, see J. R. Donahue, "Biblical Perspectives on Justice," in Haughey, ed. *Faith That Does Justice,* 68–112ff, S. C. Mott, *Biblical Ethics and Social Change* (New York: Oxford University, 1982), and J. Reumann, *"Righteousness" in the New Testament, "Justification" in the U.S. Lutheran–Roman Catholic Dialog,* with responses by J. A. Fitzmyer and J. D. Quinn (Philadelphia: Fortress; New York/Ramsey/Toronto: Paulist, 1982).

[8] Questions of wealth and poverty in the Bible have received

a great deal of attention in recent years by biblical scholars. Some of the important works are: J. Dupont and A. George, ed. *La pauvreté évangélique* (Paris: Cerf, 1971); M. Hengel, *Property and Riches in the Early Church* (Philadelphia: Fortress, 1974); L. Johnson, *Sharing Possessions: Mandate and Symbol of Faith* (Philadelphia: Fortress, 1981); D.L. Mealand, *Poverty and Expectation in the Gospels* (London: SPCK, 1980); W. Pilgrim, *Good News to the Poor: Wealth and Poverty in Luke-Acts* (Minneapolis: Augsburg, 1981) and W. Stegemann, *The Gospel and the Poor* (Philadelphia: Fortress, 1984).

[9] Stegemann, *Gospel and the Poor*, pp. 38–39.

[10] John Paul II, Address to Workers at São Paulo, Origins, 10:9 (July 31, 1980), p. 139, and Homily at Yankee Stadium, Origins, 9:19, nos. 7–8, pp. 311–312.

[11] Radio Message, Sept. 11, 1962, in The Pope Speaks, 8, 8 (Spring, 1963), p. 396.

[12] *Octogesima Adveniens*, 23.

[13] Homily at Yankee Stadium, Origins, 9:19, no. 3, p. 311.

[14] In his careful study, *Option for the Poor: A Hundred Years of Vatican Social Teaching* (Dublin: Gil and MacMillan; Maryknoll, N.Y.: Orbis, 1983), Donal Dorr has shown that concern for the marginal and for those suffering economic injustice has been the constant refrain of Catholic social teaching since Leo XIII. On the use of this term at Puebla, see "Evangelization in Latin America's Present and Future." Final Document of the Third General Conference of the Latin American Episcopate (Puebla, Mexico, Jan. 27–Feb. 13, 1979), esp. Part IV, Ch. 1, "A Preferential Option for the Poor," in J. Eagleson and P. Scharper, eds., *Puebla and Beyond* (Maryknoll, N.Y.: Orbis, 1979), pp. 264–267.

[15] Address to Bishops of Brazil, 6.9, Origins, 10:9 (July 31, 1980), p. 135.

[16] Address to Workers at São Paulo, 4, Origins, *ibid.*, p. 138.

[17] Venerable Bede, Homily 21, *Corpus Christianorum Series Latina*, 122, no. 149.

[18] Apostolic letter *Salvifici Doloris* ("The Christian Meaning of Suffering"), 28–30, (Feb. 11, 1984), Origins, 13:37 (Feb. 23, 1984), pp. 622–623.

II. ETHICAL NORMS FOR ECONOMIC LIFE

[1] See Pastoral Constitution, 44; Declaration on Religious Freedom, 1.

[2] "On Human Work," 6.

[3] *Ibid.,* 10.

[4] "Peace on Earth," 18–22; see "On Human Work," 18 and 19.

[5] John Winthrop, "A Model of Christian Charity," in Perry Miller and Thomas H. Johnson, eds., *The Puritans,* vol. I, rev. ed. (New York: Harper Torchbooks, 1963), p. 198. The spelling in the quoted text has been modernized.

[6] See 1971 Synod of Bishops, "Justice in the World," 10 and 16, and *Octogesima Adveniens,* 15.

[7] The phrase is that of Joan Costello from an unpublished paper, "The Child's Understanding of the Adult Social World" presented at a conference on "Justice for the Child within the Family Context," Loyola University of Chicago, March 26, 1979.

[8] Pius XI, *Divini Redemptoris,* 51. John A. Ryan has explained Pius XI's notion of social justice in the following way: "Social justice impels both individuals and public officials to promote the common good; that is, the common welfare taken distributively as well as collectively; the good of the community, not only as a unified entity, but as composed of social groups and individuals." *Distributive Justice, op. cit.:* p. 188.

[9] "Justice in the World," 9.

[10] Pastoral Constitution, 29.

[11] Address on Christian Unity in a Technological Age, Toronto, Sept. 14, 1984, in Origins, 14:16 (Oct. 4, 1984), p. 248.

[12] Rerum Novarum, 62; see no. 9.

[13] See "On Human Work," 19.

[14] "On Human Work," 20.

[15] Ibid., 20.

[16] Ibid.

[17] Address to Businessmen and Economic Managers, Milan, May 22, 1983 in L'Osservatore Romano, weekly edition in English, June 20, 1983, p. 9, no. 1.

[18] "On Human Work," 12.

[19] See Rerum Novarum, 10, 15 and 36.

[20] Mater et Magistra, 109.

[21] See Rerum Novarum, 65 and 66.

[22] Mater et Magistra, 115.

[23] See John Paul II's Opening Address at the Puebla Conference, Puebla, Mexico, Jan. 28, 1979, in John Eagleson and Philip Scharper, eds., Puebla and Beyond (Maryknoll, N.Y.: Orbis, 1979), p. 67.

[24] "On the Development of Peoples," 23.

[25] "On Human Work," 14.

[26] Octogesima Adveniens, 24. See also Pastoral Constitution, 74.

[27] See "Peace on Earth," 63–64.

[28] Quadragesimo Anno, 79.

[29] Message of John Paul II to UNCTAD VI in International Economics: Interdependence and Dialogue, Contributions of the Holy See on the Occasion of UNCTAD VI (Vatican City: Pontifical Commission Justice and Peace, 1984), p. 6.

[30] National Conference of Catholic Bishops, "The Challenge of Peace" (Washington, D.C.: USCC, 1983), no. 236.

[31] "On the Development of Peoples," 19.

[32] "Justice in the World," 40.

[33] See National Conference of Catholic Bishops, "Health and Health Care," November 1981. Office of Publishing Services, USCC, Washington, D.C.

III. EMPLOYMENT

[1] See Article 10 of the "Charter of the Rights of the Family," issued by the Holy See, Origins, 13:27, Dec. 15, 1983, p. 461; and "On Human Work," 19.

[2] U.S. Department of Labor, Bureau of Labor Statistics, *The Employment Situation* (September 1984), Table A-1.

[3] *Ibid.*

[4] Isabel V. Sawhill and Charles F. Stone state the prevailing view among economists this way: "High employment is usually defined as the rate of unemployment consistent with no additional inflation, a rate currently believed by many, but not all, economists to be in the neighborhood of 6 percent." "The Economy: The Key to Success," in John L. Palmer and Isabel V. Sawhill, eds., *The Reagan Record: An Assessment of America's Changing Domestic Priorities* (Cambridge, Mass.: Bollinger, 1984), p. 72. See also Stanley Fischer and Rudiger Dornbusch, *Economics* (New York: McGraw-Hill, 1983), pp. 731–743.

[5] Richard M. Cohn, "The Consequences of Unemployment on Evaluation of Self." Doctoral dissertation, Department of Psychology, University of Michigan, 1977; John A. Garraty, *Unemployment in History: Economic Thought and Public Policy* (New York: Harper and Row, 1978); Harry Maurer, *Not Working: An Oral History of the Unemployed* (New York: Holt, Rinehart and Winston, 1979).

[6] Garraty, *Unemployment in History.*

[7] K.L. Scholzman and S. Verba, "The New Unemployment: Does It Hurt?" Public Policy, 1978, p. 337.

[8] See J.R. Kesselman, "Work Relief Programs in the Great Depression" in J.L. Palmer, ed., *Creating Jobs: Public Employment Programs and Wage Subsidies* (Washington, D.C.: Brookings Institution, 1978), pp. 153–229.

[9] See the essays by Baily and Tobin and by Kesselman in Palmer, ed., *Creating Jobs,* pp. 43–76 and 153–229. See also Committee for Economic Development, *Training and Jobs in Action: Case Studies in Private Sector Initiatives for the Hard to Employ* (New York: Committee for Economic Development, 1978); Paul T. Pryde Jr., "Incentives to Economic Development," in Jack A. Meyer, ed., *Meeting Human Needs: Toward a New Public Philosophy* (Washington, D.C.: American Enterprise Institute, 1982), pp. 201–212.

[10] The problem of rapid turnover is discussed by D.S. Hamermesh, "Subsidies for Jobs in the Private Sector," in Palmer, *Creating Jobs,* p. 90.

[11] W.L. Birch, "Who Creates Jobs?" The Public Interest, 65 (Fall, 1981), pp. 3–14.

IV. POVERTY

[1] U.S. Bureau of the Census, Current Population Reports, Series P-60, No. 145, *Money Income and Poverty Status of Families and Persons in the United States: 1983,* U.S. Government Printing Office, 1984, p. 20.

[2] U.S. Bureau of the Census, Technical Paper No. 52, *Estimates of Poverty Including the Value of Non-Cash Benefits: 1983,* p. 2, Table I.

[3] U.S. Department of Housing and Urban Development,

Office of Policy Development and Research, *A Report to the Secretary on the Homeless and Emergency Shelters,* May 1984; Mary Ellen Hombs and Mitch Snyder, *Homelessness in America: A Forced March to Nowhere,* Washington, D.C., Community for Creative Non-Violence, December 1982.

[4] Center on Budget and Policy Priorities, *Soup Lines and Food Baskets: A Survey of Increased Participation in Emergency Food Programs,* Washington, D.C., May 1983, pp. 5–6; U.S. Conference of Mayors, *Status Report: Emergency Food, Shelter, and Energy Programs in 20 Cities,* Washington, D.C., January 1984, p. 2.

[5] Massachusetts Department of Public Health, *Massachusetts Nutrition Survey,* Boston, 1983.

[6] Children's Defense Fund, *American Children in Poverty,* Washington, D.C., 1984.

[7] G.J. Duncan, *Years of Poverty, Years of Plenty: The Changing Economic Fortunes of American Workers and Their Families* (Ann Arbor, Mich.: Institute for Social Research, University of Michigan, 1984).

[8] *Ibid.,* Table 2.1. The persistently poor are defined as those with incomes below the poverty line for eight of the 10 years studied.

[9] *Ibid.,* p. 50.

[10] *Ibid.,* pp. 53–55.

[11] U.S. House of Representatives, subcommittees on oversight and public assistance and unemployment compensation, Committee on Ways and Means, *Background Material on Poverty,* Washington, D.C., October 1983.

[12] The National Urban League, *The Status of Black America 1984,* New York, January 1984.

[13] Arthur I. Blaustein, *The American Promise,* New Brunswick, N.J., 1982, pp. 8–14.

[14] U.S. Bureau of the Census, Series T-23, No. 124, *Special*

Study Child Support and Alimony: 1981 Current Population Report (Washington, D.C., 1981).

[15] See, for example, R. Edmonds, "Programs of School Improvement: An Overview," Educational Leadership, December 1982, pp. 4–11; Wilbur Brookover *et. al., School Social Systems and Student Achievement: Schools Can Make a Difference* (New York: Praeger, 1979); and Northwest Regional Educational Laboratory, *Effective Schooling Practices: A Research Synthesis,* Portland, Ore., undated, circa 1983. There is still considerable debate about what, precisely, is the best strategy for promoting more effective schooling, but studies to date provide some basis for optimism about the outcomes of such reforms.

[16] Duncan, *op. cit.*

[17] M. Rein and L. Rainwater, "Patterns of Welfare Use." Social Service Review, 52, 1978, pp. 511–534; Duncan, *op. cit.*

[18] *Ibid.*

[19] See H.R. Rodgers Jr., *The Cost of Human Neglect: America's Welfare Failure* (Armonk, N.Y.: W.E. Sharpe Inc., 1982); C.T. Waxman, *The Stigma of Poverty,* 2nd ed. (New York: Pergamon Press, 1983), especially Ch. 5; and S.A. Levitan and C.M. Johnson, *Beyond the Safety Net: Reviving the Promise of Opportunity in America,* Cambridge, Mass.: Ballinger, 1984.

[20] Center on Social Welfare Policy and Law, *Beyond the Myths: The Families Helped by the AFDC Program.* New York, 1983.

V. FOOD AND AGRICULTURE

[1] Data gathered in 1984 suggests that by early 1985 as much as one-third of all family-sized commercial farms will be in some degree of financial difficulty. As many as 93,000 farms will be technically insolvent or moving rapidly toward insol-

vency. Another 136,000 will be facing serious financial problems. "The Current Condition of Farmers and Farm Lenders," Ag. Info. Bulletin No. 490. Washington, D.C.: U.S. Department of Agriculture Economic Research Service, March 1985, pp. viii–x.

[2] The nature of this transformation and its implications have been addressed previously by the USCC Committee on Social Development and World Peace in a February 1979 statement titled "The Family Farm," and again in May 1980 by the bishops of the Midwest in a joint pastoral letter titled "Strangers and Guests: Toward Community in the Heartland."

[3] "Economic Indicators of the Farm Sector: Income and Balance Sheet Statistics, 1983," ECIFS 3-3. Washington, D.C.: U.S. Department of Agriculture Economic Research Service, September 1984.

[4] There is growing public concern over absentee and corporate ownership of farmland. A major U.S. Department of Agriculture study of farmland ownership conducted in 1978 found that non-family corporations constitute less than 3 percent of land owners but own more than 11 percent of the land. Absentee ownership by retired farmers or white-collar and blue-collar owners constitute 38 percent of farm and ranch land. Marion Clawson, "Ownership Patterns of Natural Resources in America: Implications for Distribution of Wealth and Income." Washington, D.C.: Resources for the Future, Summer 1983.

[5] The impact of federal commodity and tax programs on the structure of agriculture is explored in Tweeten, "Causes and Consequences," *op. cit.,* and in "A Time to Choose: Summary Report on the Structure of Agriculture." Washington, D.C.: U.S. Department of Agriculture, January 1981.

[6] A recent comprehensive study of the structure of American agriculture by the U.S. Department of Agriculture reported that, if current trends are allowed to continue untempered,

"This will become a nation of fewer and fewer farm operations of ever-increasing size. There is little or nothing to be gained from allowing these tendencies free rein, in terms of the society's expressed goals for the food and agriculture system. Indeed allowing these trends free rein would instead produce, in many respects, results which are the opposite of those sought by our society." "A Time to Choose," *op. cit.*, p. 148.

VI. A NEW AMERICAN EXPERIMENT: COLLABORATING TO SHAPE THE ECONOMY

[1] See Sheldon S. Wolin, *Politics and Vision: Continuity and Innovation in Western Political Thought* (Boston: Little, Brown, 1960), Chap. 10; Michael Walzer, *Obligations: Reflections on Disobedience, War, and Citizenship* (New York: Simon and Schuster, 1970), Chap. 10. Their views parallel that of Paul VI in *Octogesima Adveniens*, 24.

[2] For different analyses along these lines with quite different starting points see Charles E. Lindblom, *Politics and Markets* (New York: Basic Books, 1977), esp. pp. 346–348; Lester Thurow, *The Zero-Sum Society* (New York: Basic Books, 1980), esp. Chap. 1; George F. Will, *Statecraft as Soulcraft: What Government Does* (New York: Simon and Schuster, 1982), esp. Chap. 6; Edward S. Herman, *Corporate Control, Corporate Power* (New York: Cambridge University Press, 1981), esp. Chap. 5.

[3] For diverse formulations of this viewpoint see Robert Bellah, *The Broken Covenant: American Civil Religion in Time of Trial* (New York: Seabury, 1975); Martin Carnoy, Derek Shearer and Russell Rumberger, *A New Social Contract* (New York: Harper and Row, 1983); Amitai Etzioni, *An Immodest*

Agenda: Reconstructing America Before the Twenty-First Century
(New York: McGraw-Hill, 1983); George C. Lodge, *The New
American Ideology* (New York: Alfred A. Knopf, 1975);
Douglas Sturm, "Corporations, Constitutions and Cove-
nants," Journal of the American Academy of Religion, 41
(1973), pp. 331–355; Roberto Mangabeira Unger, *Knowledge
and Politics* (New York: Free Press, 1975); George F. Will,
Statecraft as Soulcraft: What Government Does.

[4] For analysis of the relevant papal teachings on institutions
of collaboration and partnership see John Cronin, *Catholic
Social Principles: The Social Teaching of the Catholic Church
Applied to American Economic Life* (Milwaukee: Bruce, 1950),
Chap. 7; Oswald von Nell-Breuning, *Reorganization of Social
Economy: The Social Encyclical Developed and Explained,* trans.
Bernard W. Dempsey (Milwaukee: Bruce, 1936), Chaps. 10–
12; Jean-Yves Calvez and Jacques Perrin, *The Church and
Social Justice,* trans. J.R. Kirwan (Chicago: Regnery, 1961),
Chap. 19.

[5] *Rerum Novarum,* 28.

[6] "On Human Work," 12.

[7] *Quadragesimo Anno* states the basic norm on which this
conclusion is directly based: "It is wholly false to ascribe to
property alone or to labor alone whatever has been obtained
through the combined effort of both, and it is wholly unjust
for either, denying the efficacy of the other, to arrogate to
itself whatever has been produced" (No. 53).

[8] "On Human Work," 20. This point was well made by John
Cronin 25 years ago: "Even if most injustice and exploitation
were removed, unions would still have a legitimate place.
They are the normal voice of labor, necessary to organize
social life for the common good. There is positive need for
such organization today, quite independently of any social
evils which may prevail. Order and harmony do not happen;

they are the fruit of conscious and organized effort. While we may hope that the abuses which occasioned the rise of unions may disappear, it does not thereby follow that unions will have lost their function. On the contrary, they will be freed from unpleasant, even though temporarily necessary, tasks and able to devote all their time and efforts to a better organization of social life." *Catholic Social Principles,* p. 418.

[9] A number of commentators have recently echoed the basic insight of the principle of subsidiarity in discussing efforts of this sort. See Peter L. Berger and Richard John Neuhaus, *To Empower People: The Role of Mediating Structures in Public Policy* (Washington, D.C.: American Enterprise Institute, 1977); Michael Novak, *Democracy and Mediating Structures: A Theological Inquiry* (Washington, D.C.: American Enterprise Institute, 1980).

[10] See U.S. Small Business Administration, 1978 Annual Report (Washington, D.C.: Government Printing Office, 1979).

[11] For examples and analysis of different meanings of economic planning see Naomi Caiden and Aaron Wildavsky, *Planning and Budgeting in Poor Countries* (New York: Wiley, 1974); Robert Dahl and Charles E. Lindblom, *Politics, Economics and Welfare: Planning and Politico-Economic Systems Resolved into Basic Social Processes* (Chicago: Univ. of Chicago Press, 1976); Stephen S. Cohen, *Modern Capitalist Planning: The French Model* (Berkeley: Univ. of California Press, 1977); Albert Waterston, *Development Planning: Lessons of Experience* (Baltimore: Johns Hopkins Press, 1965); Aaron Wildavsky, "If Planning Is Everything, Maybe It's Nothing," Policy Sciences, 4 (1973), pp. 127–153; Gar Alperovitz and Jeff Faux, *Rebuilding America* (New York: Pantheon, 1984).

[12] "On the Development of Peoples," 3.

our discussion of these themes in "The Challenge of d's Promise and Our Response," 259–273.

VII. UNITED STATES AND THE WORLD ECONOMY

[1] Instruction on Certain Aspects of the Theology of Liberation, I:6.

[2] See earlier discussion of "Ethical Norms for Economic Life" in this document, pp. 217–246.

[3] The World Bank, whose formal title is International Bank for Reconstruction and Development, is in fact a family of institutions, including also the International Development Association and the International Finance Corporation. The regional banks include the Inter-American Development Bank, the Asian Development Bank and the African Development Fund.

[4] U.N. Center on Transnational Corporations maintains current statistics on these institutions; for a general description of their role in the international economic system, see Ronald Muller and Richard Barnet, *Global Reach* (New York: Simon and Schuster, 1974).

[5] The Conference Board, *Multinational Corporations and Developing Countries,* Report No. 767 (New York: Conference Board, 1979).

[6] Although there is an increasing number of such corporations based in developing countries, the main centers of international corporate power remain in the industrialized world, particularly the United States.

[7] Erb and Kallab, *op. cit.;* see also Brandt, Tinbergen and the Charter of the Economic Rights and Duties of Nations, U.N. General Assembly, 1974.

[8] Letter May 25, 1983, to Gamani Corea, Secretary General of U.N. Conference on Trade and Development.

[9] The Commission on Security and Economic Assistance: A Report to the Secretary of State (Washington, November 1983)—the Carlucci Commission.

[10] USCC, "The Challenge of Peace," 1983, p. 260.

[11] World Development Report 1984, Tables 9–14.

[12] Overseas Development Council, Agenda 1983, Tables A-4, A-5.

[13] "Terms of trade" refers to the ratio of imports to exports; if the cost of the former exceeds the earnings from the latter, the terms of trade are considered adverse to the exporting country.

[14] *Populorum Progressio, ibid.* The pope said that "the principle of free trade, by itself, is no longer adequate for regulating international agreements."

[15] See earlier discussion of "Ethical Norms for Economic Life" in this document, pp. 217–246.

[16] *Ibid.*

[17] Ruther Leger Sivard, *World Military and Social Expenditures 1983* (Washington: World Priorities, 1983), p. 23.

[18] Oct. 6, 1979, *The Social Teaching of John Paul II*, No. 6, p. 29: Pontifical Commission Justice and Peace, 1980.

CONCLUSION

[1] See Pastoral Constitution, 36.

[2] Pastoral Constitution, 33 and 10.

[3] Dogmatic Constitution on the Church, 40.

[4] See "On Human Work," Part 5, for a very helpful discussion of "Elements for a Spirituality of Work."

SOURCES

The American Apostolate—American Catholics in the Twentieth Century
Edited by Leo Richard Ward, C.S.C.
The Newman Press, Westminster, Maryland, 1952.

American Catholics and the Social Question—1865–1900
James Edmund Roohan
Arno Press, A New York Times Company, New York, 1976.

Bishops and People
By Members of the Catholic Theological Faculty of Tubingen Gunter Biemer, Hans Kung, Johannes Neumann, Peter Stockmeier and others with Bishop Josef Schoiswohl and Leonard Swidler
Edited and Translated by Leonard Swidler and Arlene Swidler
The Westminster Press, Philadelphia.

Catholic Bishops—A Memoir
John Tracy Ellis
Michael Glazier, Inc., Wilmington, Delaware.

*The Catholic Church in the Modern World, A Survey
from the French Revolution to the Present*
E. E. Y. Hales
Hanover House, Garden City, New York, 1958.

*The First Council of the Vatican: The American
Experience*
James Hennessey, S.J.
Herder and Herder.

Goethe's World As Seen in Letters and Memoirs
Edited by Berthold Biermann
Books for Libraries Press, Freeport, New York.

*The Great Crisis in American Catholic History,
1895–1900*
Thomas Timothy McAvoy, C.S.C.
Henry Regnery Company, Chicago, 1957.

*The Life of James Cardinal Gibbons: Archbishop of
Baltimore, 1834–1921*
John Tracy Ellis
2 vols., Bruce, Milwaukee, 1952.

*The Mind of John Paul II—Origins of His Thought
and Action*
George Hunston Williams
Seaburg, New York.

*The Ministry of Bishops: Papers from The Collegeville
Assembly*
The Bishops' Assembly for Prayer and Reflection
    iscopal Ministry, June 13–23, 1982—St.

John's University, Collegeville, Minnesota,
National Conference of Catholic Bishops.

Newman and Gladstone: The Vatican Decrees
With an Introduction by Alvan S. Ryan
University of Notre Dame Press, 1962.

Pastoral Letters of the American Hierarchy, 1792–1970
Edited by Hugh J. Nolan
Huntington, Indiana, 1971.

*The Pursuit of a Just Social Order, Policy Statements
of the U.S. Catholic Bishops, 1966–1980*
J. Bryan Benestad, Foreword by Avery Dulles, S.J.
Ethics and Public Policy Center, Washington,
D.C.

*The Roman Question, Extracts from the Despatches of
Odo Russell from Rome, 1858–1870*
London, Chapman and Hall, 37 Essex Street,
WC2.

Right Reverend New Dealer, John A. Ryan
Francis L. Broderick
The Macmillan Company, New York;
Collier–Macmillan Ltd., London.

Vatican Diary 1962
*A Protestant Observes the First Session of Vatican
Council II*
United Church Press, Philadelphia—Boston.

ABOUT THE AUTHOR

EUGENE KENNEDY, Professor of Psychology at Loyola University, is a longtime student and observer of the American Catholic Church. In addition to his writings on spiritual and psychological subjects, Kenndy is an award-winning biographer and novelist whose works include *Himself!*, a biography of Mayor Richard J. Daley of Chicago, and the novel *Father's Day*.